what it is and why it matters

children's
spirituality

D0910987

Other titles in this series

Employing Youth and Children's Workers
A guide for churches

Paul Godfrey and Nic Sheppard

Children and Bereavement
2nd edition

Wendy Duffy

Not Just Sunday
Setting up and running mid-week clubs for children

Margaret Withers

Rural Children, Rural Church
Mission opportunities in the countryside

Rona Orme

Special Children, Special Needs
Integrating children with disabilities and special needs into your church

Simon Bass

Where Two or Three
Help and advice for churches with few or no children

Margaret Withers

what it is and why it matters

children's spirituality

Rebecca Nye

CHURCH HOUSE
PUBLISHING

Church House Publishing

Church House

Great Smith Street

London SW1P 3AZ

ISBN 978 0 7151 4027 7

Published 2009 by Church House Publishing

The opinions expressed in this book are those of the author and
do not necessarily reflect the official policy of the General Synod
or The Archbishops' Council of the Church of England.

The Scripture quotations contained herein are from *The New
Revised Standard Version of the Bible*, Anglicized Edition, copyright
© 1989, 1995 by the Division of Christian Education of the National
Council of the Churches of Jesus Christ in the United States of
America, and are used by permission. All rights reserved.

Printed in England by CPI William Clowes Beccles NR34 7TL

Contents

Foreword

All human beings are spiritual people. This is the way God has made us. Children are not only no less spiritual than adults, they are often, it appears, more open to their spiritual reality. Rebecca Nye has worked tirelessly for many years now not simply researching into Children's Spirituality but also seeking to encourage all of us to take it far more seriously. She has been a wonderful advocate for making sure that our practice in churches, schools and wider society really does take children and their spirituality utterly seriously (though with a great sense of fun, play and wonder). This latest book leaves us all further indebted to Rebecca for her joyful, thorough, imaginative and playful work.

Here we find opening chapters which are straightforward and plain speaking on the reality and nature of children's spirituality. She outlines different ways that 'spirituality' and 'children's spirituality' are understood and explored. Then, extremely helpfully, Rebecca encourages the reader to engage with her/his own childhood as one key way of engaging with the spirituality of the children amongst whom we serve. She does so with a real awareness that this will not be an easy task for most of us; so she offers ideas and exercises which help us take the journey. These opening chapters help us explore, and 'understand' the very nature of children's spirituality.

Then Rebecca moves us all on to take seriously how we work in practice with each child's spiritual nature, fascination and development. Her general S.P.I.R.I.T principles (Space, Process, Imagination, Relationship, Intimacy, Trust) are extremely helpful, and lay an excellent foundation for her later more specific exploration of Prayer, the Bible, and Imagery.

Her final chapter of 'Frequently Asked Questions' is full of thoughtful insight into a range of questions that are indeed frequently raised whenever dealing with people who work with children.

I have found reading this book enriching, encouraging, refreshing and challenging. It not only instructs and equips about children's spirituality, and how adults work alongside children with this reality, it also stretches and enriches our own spirituality, and relationship with God. For at the end of the day 'spirituality' is not a bland ethereal idea; it is a human and divine reality. Our spirituality is rooted in God, who he is and how he has made us. 'Children's spirituality' is a joyous God-given reality in which we should all revel and rejoice.

So I encourage all who pick up this book to read it not simply as an intellectual exercise but a spiritual one. Create Space to read it reflectively; engage in the Process of the book; use your Imagination; enter into Relationship with Rebecca through the book, and consider relating with others as you do so. Allow the whole process to develop appropriate Intimacy in your own relationship with God and others, especially children. As you do this Trust will deepen; trust in the living God; trust in others and trust in yourself. Allow the experience of engaging with the book to shape you, and above all shape how you listen to and work alongside children, and their amazing spirituality.

+ Paul Butler, Bishop of Southampton

Acknowledgements

A book about children's spirituality must first acknowledge the contribution children have made to the ideas and insights therein. In my case, these include the children who I've encountered in research projects, in churches, in schools and of course my own children, Louisa, Isaac and Thomas. The irony of writing a book about attending to children's spirituality that sometimes left my own children pitifully enquiring, 'But when will it be teatime?' was an important reality check.

Any claim I might have to expertise in this area is set within a context of wise and experienced colleagues. The company of these colleagues and friends has provided the crucible for mixing and creating a way of focusing on children's spirituality specifically for the Church. Many of these colleagues are, or were, diocesan advisers, including Peter Privett, Gill Ambrose, Mary Hawes, Richard Burge and Alison Seaman.

Godly Play has clearly offered a huge gift by turning respect for children's spirituality into practice, so I am deeply grateful to Jerome and Thea Berryman too.

The Sir Halley Stewart Trust generously supported me in the early stage of writing; and Tracey Messenger, the commissioning editor at Church House Publishing, deserves sainthood for her patience, as well as earning my gratitude for her guidance throughout. And, Andrew, thanks for everything.

Introduction

What this book is about

This book is about children's spirituality: what it is, why it's important to protect and nurture it, and how to put spirituality first in your practice.

Many people say, 'Oh, that must be interesting', when they hear that children's spirituality is being discussed, and maybe that's why you have picked up this book. But this is a topic that is much more than 'interesting': vital practical matters are at stake here too. This book offers guidance about the choices made in churches and homes that can stimulate, or mutilate, children's spirituality.

This book focuses on children's spirituality in three ways:

- childhood as a natural source of spirituality;
- ways to help children value and express their spirituality;
- discerning the role of Christian nurture and worship in early spiritual development.

When spirituality is given the attention it deserves, we can make a vital and positive contribution to children's lives. The case made here is that spirituality is a very important reality in childhood – not just a nice idea. If our practices and thinking about children do not take this into account, we run the risk of making significant mistakes, even of damaging their spiritual lives.

It is not easy to pinpoint what spirituality means, especially in view of all the different phases of childhood. So this book offers an introductory guide to its main features, drawing in particular on recent research with children, psychological theories of child development and Christian writing about childhood. A key feature explored in these pages is the rich natural spiritual capacity of childhood – spirituality as something 'already there', to be cherished, rather than something to be added on.

This means learning to view spirituality as something we expect in every child, rather than something unusual or precocious. Taking children's spirituality seriously can significantly influence our view of children. It can help us both to embrace the reality that children are made in God's image, that they are already spiritually switched on, and also to challenge the view that children come in a kind of 'kit version' that we must make into a 'God-compatible' model. Sometimes we seem to behave as if spiritual life can only begin once a child has been filled up, by us, with enough religious knowledge. In this book, facilitating children's growing fluency in religious understanding is seen as enriching the spiritual life they already enjoy.

Who the book is for

From our earliest moments as infants, we need to derive meaning from experience. This book is for anyone who feels that Christian language has a distinctive contribution to offer on how we make meaning in our lives. In particular, this book is for those who influence situations involving children. It is for parents, clergy, children's work leaders, teachers and many more. Indeed, it might be easier to make a list of people for whom this topic is irrelevant – such as anyone who was never a child or anyone who only relates to others who've never been children.

Many of the practical examples and suggestion given here focus on how churches work with children, and on how to approach ministry with, to and by children in a spirituality supportive way. But the larger implications, such as how all Christians might view childhood differently in the light of the child's spiritual capacity, make this topic relevant for every member of your congregation. Indeed, it might be enlightening to use this book as a basis for discussion in a home or study group.

How this book can help you

An understanding of children's spirituality challenges a number of practices in children's work, so this book is a guide to thinking about why you do what you do. The book suggests that spirituality is often *not* at the heart of the choices we make about ministry with children, and that sometimes our work with children is in danger of being anything but spiritual.

Here you will find help for thinking critically about your choices, as well as useful suggestions about what spirituality-focused practice can look like in different situations: in worship, teaching, Bible reading and prayer, and in your everyday relationships with children.

Being able to connect with and draw on our *own* childlike spiritual qualities is clearly at the heart of Christian spiritual growth – to enter the kingdom of heaven each of us must become like a child. So, this book may also help you to reflect on how your spirituality was cherished (or neglected) as a child, and the effect that's had on your faith journey.

The shape of this book

Chapter 1 contains a brief introduction to spirituality in general before going on to consider definitions of children's spirituality.

Chapter 2 examines whether taking time to consider children's spirituality in work with children is something of a luxury, the 'icing on the cake', or a necessity.

In Chapter 3 we look first of all at ways of recognizing children's spirituality by getting in touch with our own spirituality, before moving on to consider how to get in touch with the spirituality of the children with whom we work.

Chapter 4 introduces some general principles and criteria that may be used to assess whether or not our work with children is supporting their spirituality.

Chapter 5 considers ways of supporting children's spirituality with reference to the particular practices of prayer and Bible reading.

In Chapter 6 we look at some intersections between Christian theology and children's spirituality.

Chapter 7 gives answers to some frequently asked questions about children's spirituality.

If you would like to take things further, there is a further reading list and list of resources at the end of the book.

1 Children's spirituality: what is it?

What is spirituality?

delighting in all things
being absorbed in the present moment
not too attached to 'self' and
eager to explore boundaries of 'beyond' and 'other'
searching for meaning
discovering purpose
open to more?[1]

Spirituality is like a bird; if you hold it too tightly, it chokes; if you hold it too loosely, it flies away. Fundamental to spirituality is the absence of force.

Rabbi Hugo Gryn

Spirituality is not something that likes to be confined in words – which makes writing (and reading) about it horribly difficult! It is more 'felt–sense', drawing on non-verbal insights, vision, sound, touch and so on. It can be a powerful kind of *knowing* that is less worried about proving how you know.

Because it is powerful, literally in*spir*ing, spirituality also shapes our ways of *being*. This far-reaching combination of deeply motivated knowing and being ends up in what is referred to in the monastic traditions as a 'rule of life', that is, it potentially affects everything.

This gives spirituality an interesting relationship with verbal language and, of course, religious language. Attempts to define or theorize spirituality are often frustrating. Perhaps this is because a single definition can only capture one part of the whole picture, or because when a definition tries to take in the whole picture you need to stand so far back to see it that there is not much to focus on!

You might already have a favourite way of defining or thinking about spirituality. If so, it will be useful to be aware of that as you read on. Or you could try now to make up a definition – and perhaps discover how hard it is to get the words to say what you feel about this topic. You could also begin making a collection of other people's ways of defining spirituality, starting from the few given below, and thinking about what you like and dislike about these.

Spirituality is . . .

From theologians

> living fully with nothing excluded from our hearts
>
> Gerald May

> each believer making his or her own engagement with the questioning at the heart of faith . . . constantly allowed to challenge the fixed assumptions of religiosity
>
> Rowan Williams

> the search for God in response to God's search for us
>
> Jo Anne Taylor

a conscious involvement in the project of life integration
through self transcendence toward the ultimate value
one perceives

Sandra Schneiders

From educators

spirituality ranges from sensing of divine presence to the
recognition of a heightened quality in an event or encounter
and a response of awe and wonder

David Dixon

signals of transcendence that are normal aspects of life but all
at odds with a materialistic understanding of the world, they
point to something other – something more . . . can lead
people to an awareness of religion

Brenda Watson

the sense making activity that both children and adults
necessarily carry out as a result of the life experiences they
encounter

Clive Erricker

From psychologists

an awareness, response or ability to reflect on areas which are
beyond those of individual/ego interest, that is not concerning
the individual's own survival or fortune. To this extent spiritual
interests could be termed (apparently) pointless ones

Margaret Donaldson

a belief that there is an unseen order, and that our supreme
good lies in harmoniously adjusting ourselves thereto

William James

Just jargon?

Words connected to 'spirituality' often crop up in everyday conversation:

keep your spirits up

she gave a spirited performance

that was mean-spirited

I don't think I've got the spirit for this anymore

that's the spirit!

(there's even a supermarket own-brand deodorant called 'Spiritual'!)

Recently it has been fashionable for many outside the Church to describe
themselves as 'spiritual, but not religious'. So when trying to work out
what spirituality means, we also need to think about how far we need
this to be tied to formal Christian language. Or whether the 'Christian'
element is more about the outworkings in practice, and not the words
or concepts in themselves.

Christians are certainly used to hearing spirit-related words all the time –
in psalms, in choruses and in prayer. Again and again we refer both to
God's Spirit and our own spirit:

'. . . and the fellowship of the Holy Spirit'

'The Lord be with you. And with thy spirit'

'My spirit faints within me' (Psalm 143.4)

This 'everydayness' makes it hard to get spirituality into focus. It's a struggle to engage with critically and let it inform our practice. It seems so vague that it could mean anything – rather pointless then?

But perhaps this everyday quality is *key* to the challenge, especially the challenge of understanding spirituality in childhood. Language connected to spirituality is everywhere, reminding us how wrong it would be to shut spirituality into an exclusive box. Its everydayness in both secular and church language makes the point that spirituality is meant to entail *all* that we are called to be. So how we think about its meaning must include children.

Think and discuss . . .

Are children (of any age) in danger of being excluded by any of the definitions given here, or by ways of defining spirituality known to you?

What is children's spirituality?

The following three definitions approach children's spirituality from three perspectives:

1. A very simple definition of children's spirituality might be:

God's ways of being with children and

children's ways of being with God.

For Christians, this definition helps us to remember that children's spirituality starts with God – it is not something adults have to initiate. God and children (regardless of age or intellect) have ways of being together because this is how God created them. The difficulty comes in trying to appreciate, and support, the ambiguous forms these ways can take.

2. An evidence-based approach to defining children's spirituality lets us take things further. My research study of the varied expressions of spirituality evident in children's lives pinpointed their remarkable capacity for 'relational consciousness'.[2] This way of defining spirituality suggests some specific key features:

> Children's spirituality is an *initially natural capacity* for awareness of the sacred quality to life experiences. This awareness can be *conscious or unconscious*, and sometimes fluctuates between both, but in both cases can affect actions, feelings and thoughts. In childhood, spirituality is especially about being attracted towards 'being in relation', *responding to a call to relate* to more than 'just me' – i.e. to others, to God, to creation or to a deeper inner sense of Self. This encounter with transcendence can happen in specific experiences or moments, as well as through imaginative or reflective activity (thoughts and meaning making).

3. Or you might find this definition by analogy an easy, yet valuable, way to start thinking about what children's spirituality means:

> Children's spirituality is like a child.

- It does not usually neatly conform to accepted norms or use conventional expression.
- At first glance, it might sound like babble rather than fluent 'Christian'. It requires effort (listening) on our part to recognize what is being expressed, and to develop (not impose) a shared language.
- It surpasses compartmentalization (gets into and will use everything, not just religious material).
- It can be intense one minute and nonchalant the next. Development is rarely in a straight line or under our control.
- And often it feels like it matters to the child, but is perceived by them *not* to matter to anyone else, and not to be part of mainstream values.
- It is vulnerable, and can even die if neglected, ignored or misunderstood.

Think and discuss . . .

Look again at the three definitions of children's spirituality.

- Which do you like the most?
- What do you think is the most important element?
- What's left out?

Jesus said of children, 'Whoever welcomes one such child in my name welcomes me, and whoever welcomes me welcomes not me but the one who sent me' (Mark 9.37).

- Could any of the features in the definition 'a child's spirituality is like a child' also describe *God's* ways of being with us, that is, 'God's spirituality'?

A fair definition: including children

One thing to look out for is whether we tend to think about spirituality in ways that depend on having adult capacities, thereby excluding children or indeed others with little (religious) knowledge, or limited intellectual capacities (e.g. people with brain damage or dementia). Being fair and inclusive in how we think about spirituality is important – and not only to those who might otherwise be left out. An inclusive definition can draw attention to areas that would otherwise be overlooked, protecting us from a lopsided understanding and possibly lopsided practices.[3]

As adults, we might describe spirituality in terms of particular experiences that can reliably be recalled and talked about, for example, sensing God's presence. However, to limit children to experiences they can recall and talk about is not really fair, given that they can find it difficult to retrieve memories and put things into words. This helps us to see that a big net is needed – big enough to catch their spiritual experiences, imaginings, views, questions, play and ideas as indicative evidence of children's spirituality.

Or unfair advantage?

Spirituality might *not* be fair though: children may have the advantage! Things that adults have to work hard at in spiritual life may be quite natural and easy for children. A lot of quite ordinary childhood experience has the potential for being spiritually arousing – so maybe understanding childhood is fundamental to any attempt to understand spirituality more generally. It definitely means doing more than just squeezing children into adult spiritual criteria as a kind afterthought.

Understanding childhood involves understanding that:

- Children have a more holistic way of seeing things; they don't analyse as much, so their perception has a more *mystical* quality.

- Children are especially open and curious; they don't judge or get suspicious as much, so they have a natural capacity for *wonder.*

- Children are discovering new things daily; they don't need to steel themselves to learn, so they are comfortable with the *noetic*, which is about the feeling of being granted new understanding, a kind of surprise gift or 'aha!'.

- Children's emotional life is at least as strong as their intellectual life, they don't (or can't) hide from their feelings; so they know all about what it's like to *surrender* to forces that transcend their control.

- Children lack knowledge about many things. In every sentence there may be words they don't understand and many of the actions of those around them may be puzzling – why does Mummy disappear (to the kitchen)? *Mystery* is a close, mostly unthreatening, friend in childhood, and responding with *awe* or a *search for meaning* are everyday childhood games.

- Children easily accept that their words are not adequate to describe thoughts and feelings; they know that real worth and importance are about more than saying things. They are comfortable with the *power of what is ineffable.*

One exciting thing about trying to fathom children's spirituality is that it can help to widen and refresh our perception of spirituality in general, and perhaps our own too. Spirituality becomes more than something exclusively adult and more than any definition we are familiar with from our own Christian tradition. Sometimes it may be liberating to work out what spirituality entails by coming at it sideways – for example, using similes or a drawing. You might like to try this. Spirituality is like . . . a lover, breathing, water, a puzzle, a journey?

Think and discuss . . .

● What words or images come close to describing *your*
  spiritual life at present?

Natural for all

In recent years children's spirituality has become quite a popular topic for
research; a variety of methods have been employed and all kinds of children
have been studied – those with particular faiths and those with apparently
none. The key finding of all these studies is that spirituality is a common,
natural feature of most, probably all, children's lives. Certainly no studies have
highlighted a type of child who does not possess active spiritual capacities.
From a Christian point of view, that makes sense, since it would be difficult
to understand why some people would be created without an instinctive
capacity to respond to our Creator.

The younger the better?

Some of the research findings are even more striking. In Finland, for
example, Kalevi Tamminen found that 60 per cent of eleven-year-olds
and 80 per cent of seven-year-olds mentioned times of being aware of
God's presence. By comparison, only about 30 per cent of adults are aware
of similar experiences.[4] So spiritual awareness is especially natural and
common in childhood, and comparatively rare in adulthood.

However, understanding spiritual capacity as natural to every child's life is
often not reflected in the approach and underlying attitudes of some Christian
teaching programmes. Some still seem to treat children as spiritually empty
and passive vessels until and unless adults intervene.

This begs the question of how children's spirituality is nurtured (which later
chapters look at in more detail). We do need to ask how children's initial
inclination to recognize the sacred in their day-to-day life experiences can
be sustained. Maybe 'child protection' policies should include measures to
protect the withering of children's spiritual potential!

Think and discuss . . .

Look at a session outline used in children's work in your church (for Sunday school or a mid-week or holiday club, or a worship service that includes children).

● How do the words, activities and aims support the idea of *all* children having *naturally* rich spiritual lives in the first place?

● Do the words, activities and aims imply that children are rather empty to begin with but will be 'filled' thanks to this intervention?

Day-to-day being

In childhood we are perhaps better at simply 'being', accepting that vocation with grace. As a result, childhood spirituality is especially found in the everyday and among all that entails being a child. Maybe it is a 'rule of life' after all: is it whatever allows a child to be a child?

Jesus' approach to children seems to support the notion that spirituality refers to a basic, day-to-day state of being. While spiritual life for adult followers of Jesus required pretty radical change, children were treated differently. All children were welcomed and blessed, and at random Jesus set one child in the midst. He did not need to check first that the child singled out demonstrated a particular trait; just being a child in an everyday way was the only criterion that mattered.

Think and discuss . . .

● What helps children to be children?
● What prevents this or makes it harder?

- What does your list of helps suggest about spirituality and its nurture?
- What does your list of hindrances suggest about spiritual neglect or abuse?

Not entirely separate?

Although adult and child spirituality may have some different strengths and resources, it is unwise to treat them as two separate 'specialities': child *or* adult spirituality. They are connected in two ways.

First, a key task for adult spiritual maturity is 'to become like a child', so it won't help to have very strict import and export controls at the 'border' on the grounds that some things only belong in the land of childhood spirituality.

Secondly, children become adults and so carry forward their spiritual formation. Research has found that childhood often provides the most crucial spiritual impressions of all, the ones that could shape (or distort) all the experience of later life. Edward Robinson found that a surprising number of adults chose a childhood memory as their most important spiritual experience. Even though, as children, most of these adults had not been able to put these moments into words, these impressions still seemed potent many years later.[5]

Because spirituality can mean so many things, it is important to consider the parameters it can have. This chapter has tackled this in two ways: by looking at issues about its meanings and definitions *in general*, and by looking at some of the specific elements associated with what we mean by *children's* spirituality. Key themes have been that children's spirituality is more natural than taught; that perhaps more fertile ground for spirituality is found in childhood than in adult life; that the spirituality of childhood carries over into adulthood; and that spirituality is profoundly relational.

With a sense of *what* children's spirituality might be, the next chapter explores *why* this should matter to us and to our churches. Chapters 3 and 4 take us further inside the world of children's spirituality: its sounds and signs and the practical responses we can make to support it.

Children's Spirituality

Think and discuss . . .

- The everydayness of the spiritual – how is this true for your family life or your church life?
- Do you have any personal experience that supports the idea that children may have an 'unfair advantage' in terms of spiritual capacity?

12

2 Children's spirituality: how important is it?

Luxury or necessity?

For a long time in children's ministry no one mentioned children's spirituality very much. Because it has been a neglected topic, some untested assumptions have crept in. For example, an assumption that children are too young for 'spirituality' and need to learn about faith first; or that children don't really experience the deeper aspects of life and so won't 'get' what a lot of religious language is about, therefore, we need to make things very simple and 'just a bit of fun'.

Such neglect has made it easy for an 'infotainment' approach to dominate children's Christian nurture. This is a dangerous course to follow, both for children now and for the teenagers and adults they will become. First, it can trample on the genuine spiritual life children already have. Secondly, an infotainment, spirituality-neglecting mindset can set up long-lasting misunderstandings about faith. It can promote the idea that faith is mostly about having lots of efficiently categorized religious knowledge (Bible, doctrine, prayers, moral codes of behaviour). And it can lead to a church's role being judged in terms of how good a 'show' it provides for the congregation.

The missing link

Many Christians working with children feel a calling to this work, but curiously are dissatisfied with what they actually do. Leaders of children's work sometimes experience 'burn out'. For some people, this can be connected to a feeling that taking care of the children's nurture means missing out on opportunities for one's own spiritual growth. And despite all the effort leaders put in, a lot of children seem to grow out of faith rather than into it. Having learned the songs, the stories, and made friends, children can all too easily tread water spiritually. It is as if Christian faith has failed to engage such children on a deeper level – yet that ought to be its strength!

In our homes too there can be dissatisfaction about how to handle things. Increasingly parents and grandparents feel sensitive about 'indoctrinating' their children and worried about the risk of turning them off. Yet they have a nagging guilt, a feeling that they ought to do more to help their child discover the meaningfulness of Christian language. Getting a grip on children's spirituality may be the missing link. This may be the key to ministering to the best of our abilities with children, and finding that they can genuinely contribute to *our* spiritual life too.

Think and discuss . . .

- Identify at least three things that you really like about the work done with children in your church.
- What's your general sense of how spirituality comes into your local children's work?
- What worries you about how things are done?

Spiritual impoverishment

Children present us with so many different needs and challenges. To be told that we must be concerned for children's spirituality as well might feel like being pushed over the edge – another thing to do, another area where we don't do well enough. There are so many other compelling priorities after all.

Some children starve in a world of plenty, and too many are afflicted by disease and other effects of poverty. They can be victims of every kind of abuse; many live in difficult, unstable families; children often witness violence between their carers and towards them; they feel inadequate, depressed or are bullied at school. And there's another kind of poverty too. Over the past few decades significantly fewer children, in the UK at least, attend a church or participate in distinctively Christian education, such as a Sunday club. As a result, many children today (as well as the generation who parent them) have a religious knowledge deficiency and lack any functional sense of religious identity.

Faced with so many levels of childhood impoverishment, Christians already have an overwhelming list of important tasks to carry out in their ministry with children. So maybe concern for children's spirituality is a bit indulgent, a luxury consideration, the icing on the cake? We could be tempted to think that spirituality is only an issue when children's other needs have been met or that it might be just for 'nicely behaved' groups of children who can tolerate sitting still for a spot of contemplative discussion!

There *is* a real danger that children's spirituality may be treated in a sentimental way – with leaders regarding it as about all the 'wonderful' things children say, their innocence and their curious, naive insights. Providing spiritual nurture could also be narrowly misinterpreted as the handing out of a few discrete tasks that take some children a bit further on, such as offering opportunities to learn and use fancier ways to pray. If spiritual nurture is treated in this romanticized way, or as an 'extension activity', then concern for children's spirituality can be dismissed as fussing about 'the icing on the cake'. We need to be aware of the danger of seeing spirituality as a luxury, and recognize the sense in which it is a *basic* necessity, particularly for childhood.

The right to spiritual life

The UN Convention on the Rights of the Child (1989) refers to *spiritual rights* in four of its articles, with a further four also outlining specific religious rights. Some churches have developed a charter of rights for children, probably inspired by this model. This language of 'rights' makes quite a difference and can help us avoid merely sentimentalizing children's spirituality.

If we accept that all children have a right to spiritual well-being, it is not enough to focus fondly on just a few instances or to wait until we have the time to be charitable. Acceptance of 'rights' means that we are not simply choosing to respond out of kindness or courtesy but because it is imperative. Seeing spiritual life as a right of the child also affects the kind of response we make: we are under an obligation to meet these rights, and cannot simply be left to patronise children or value their spirituality when it suits us. When spirituality is understood in these terms, as a basic and constant feature, it should fundamentally affect everything we do. Specifically, it should challenge and inform the *content of ministry* with children, how we *think about* children and the *relationships* necessary to support this understanding.

Children's spirituality: icing on the cake?

Why it matters to us and our churches
Informing all ministry

So what if we thought of childhood spirituality as a basic ingredient of *all* ministry with children? This would mean starting from the view that spirituality is a normal capacity of childhood, not something esoteric or 'just the icing'. It would mean paying attention to the spiritual qualities (and spiritual defects) in *all* that we do, and exploring the spiritual impetus for why we do things one way and not another. For example, it could mean examining the *spiritual* merits of providing separate activities for different age groups. It could mean weighing up the *spiritual* merits of being asked to make a collage or banner, or the *spiritual* merits of beginning a children's session with 'register time' or ending with 'show and tell' to the adult congregation.

Conceived in this broader sense, attention to children's spirituality shouldn't take attention away from other tasks, such as tackling childhood poverty, evangelism or Bible teaching, rather it ought to be able give these tasks fresh impetus and vision.

Informing 'what a child is'

Childhood spirituality opens a window on to the nature of childhood in general. It can help us to be critical of ideas and practices that support views that a child is 'an empty vessel' waiting to be filled with religious knowledge or that children are like primitive (naughty) beasts and the first task of Christians is to tame them, to address their 'dodgy' moral well-being.

As one of the definitions in Chapter 1 suggested, spirituality in childhood is about children's ways of being with God and God being with them. It raises large questions about how Christians understand what 'being a person' means, and the role of childhood in life more generally. Exploring childhood from a spiritual point of view can help us move beyond the words and warm noises we sometimes make about the place of children in the Christian community. Phrases like 'children are a gift of God', 'become like a child to enter the kingdom' and 'children are made in the image of God' demand much more of us than lip service. Rather, they demand action and transformation in real children's often complicated lives.

Informing relationships
When children's spirituality is allowed a place at the *root* of what we do for children, it can exert radical consequences – changing the ways we think about things in further branches of children's ministry. The ways adults relate to children, as teachers, parents, ministers, evangelists or missionaries may need to be reconfigured, subtly or dramatically, when children's spiritual capacities are valued and theologically reflected on.

Indeed, Christians are invited to regard the simple fact of being a child as an inherently spiritual vocation. Jesus referred to children (without being specific about age) as those whose angels in heaven 'continually see the face of my Father in heaven' (Matthew 18.10). This suggests that children enjoy a spiritual perception that has nothing to do with what a child of any particular age can do or 'knows'. This is a strong hint that adults have things to learn *from* children's ways of simply being themselves, and that traditional power/authority relationships between adults and children may be misleading.

So, when children's spirituality is considered seriously, *every* aspect of calling to children's ministry and mission stands to benefit from being informed, challenged and energized. It's not just about the icing on the cake.

Spirituality: essential – to faith, childhood and being whole

| **Faith** | **Childhood** | **Being whole** |

There are at least three ways of seeing spirituality as essential. Each way makes clear the reasons why we must not try to treat it as an 'add on', something to find five minutes for in each session, or a subject that can be covered as a particular theme over a number of weeks or in one kind of activity (e.g. the prayer bit).

First, spirituality is *essential to faith*. In a car, even a full tank of petrol will make little difference if the engine has no oil, the car cannot really be driven anywhere. If faith is like that tank of petrol, then spirituality is the essential oil.

Secondly, spirituality is *essential to childhood*, not an optional extra of adulthood or something opted into by a minority. This is enshrined in law, with schools in England and Wales being required to encourage spiritual development across *all* areas of their work with children. The law is explicit that this is not just about religious education or just for faith schools, but about opportunities in every area of school life – science lessons, dinner time, school outings, behaviour policy and so on. Spirituality is seen as integral to what education and being a growing child (of any faith or none) is all about, as essential as intellectual or social development.

It is a little embarrassing that churches should have to be urged to take a leaf from secular, statutory policy and learn to treat children's spirituality in similarly essential and far-reaching terms. But it is *not* routine in most churches to reflect in such broad terms about how children are impacted by *all* the areas of church life (not only Sunday school, but worship, fellowship, leadership styles, the way space is used and shared, and mission too).

And it is particularly not routine for the key question to be, 'What are the spiritual qualities of the way we do this?'

Typically, when children's experience is considered at all, we focus on the *social* qualities. (Was it fun for them? Did they feel included or at least were they seen to be included?) Or we focus on the *intellectual* qualities. (Was the teaching point clear?) We don't ask ourselves, and often don't know even *how* to ask, about the spiritual qualities of our provision for children.

Thirdly, the spirituality of childhood is also *essential to being whole* at any stage in life. It is not just about things going on for children now. How their spirituality is recognized, allowed to develop and find expression will have direct consequences for their adult spiritual lives. For example, impressions gleaned as a child, such as that 'proper' prayer really ought to have words, or that God is specially present in beauty or in suffering, can have life-long effects on adult spiritual life. Understanding more about childhood spirituality is therefore also an important way for Christians of any age to deepen their own spiritual awareness, to become whole. It can help us recognize things that have been obstructed or encouraged in us, perhaps since childhood.

Be warned!
By now it should be clear that getting to grips with children's spirituality is not a quick fix for anything that dismays us about working with children in the church. It is a big challenge.

One reason for this is that a lot about spirituality is hard to pin down, to define (though Chapter 1 provided some pointers). And even if it were perfectly defined and enshrined in every mission statement or children's policy, this would be unlikely to make much difference in practice. What matters most is that you develop your own habits of recognizing when spirituality is, and isn't, able to flourish in your local context. This grassroots sense of meaning, based on your context and your experiences of children, will have a much higher chance of making positive changes. To get you started, later chapters in this book offer a guide to the signs and sounds of children's spirituality.

It is also a big challenge because asking questions about the spiritual qualities and intentions of our encounters with children may threaten to depose typical, sometimes 'child-friendly', church practices. When we aim for spiritual depth and growth, asking: 'Is this child-*spirituality* friendly?' we may create very different criteria for 'success' in ministry with children. Of course, anyone is free to disagree with the suggestions made here, but be prepared to find that taking children's spirituality into account often challenges practices people in church contexts associate with being 'good with children' or have considered broadly child-friendly.

Finally, looking at children's spirituality can sometimes make us feel inadequate about our own. This might be because we come to realize that our own childhood spirituality was mistreated or neglected as our faith developed, or maybe we came to faith as adults anyway, or simply can't remember much about being a child. Might this mean that we are missing a crucial piece of spiritual foundation? This is at the heart of why we need to understand children's spirituality: it is not just to do a better job of enriching their spiritual lives, but also because there are always ways in which their spirituality can enrich all of us.

Think and discuss . . .

- Have a look at some Christian picture books for children. Could the distinction between 'child-friendly' and 'child-spirituality-friendly' apply to any of them?
- How might your church be providing 'infotainment'? Does this satisfy/stimulate spiritual needs?

And if we don't take spirituality seriously?

Someday, maybe, there will exist a well informed, well considered and yet fervent conviction that the most deadly of sins is the mutilation of a child's spirit.

Eric Erikson

Taking the time to think about children's spirituality is important, but obviously not easy. There is still a lot we don't know, a lot more always to consider, as implied by the words 'someday, maybe' in the quote above. In a scientific age, we are perhaps more comfortable with things we can measure or test or that have specific objectives and outcomes. This is rarely, however, a helpful way of coming closer to what spirituality is about, for ourselves or for children.

To think about children's spirituality we need to draw on theology, scripture, child psychology, educational theory and our own personal experience. It may also require thinking critically about things 'we've always done' or things that were done to us. But, equally, getting to grips with children's spirituality may help us to recognize the skills we already possess for accompanying children in faith – as parents, teachers, friends or clergy.

Then the really hard work begins – consciously putting what we understand about children's spirituality into the heart of our practice. But if the stakes are as high as the quotation suggests, then this is certainly not an area that should be left to chance. Failure to nurture children's spirituality not only threatens to harm them, it has deadly consequences for us, both personally and for the church community.

Think and discuss . . .

- Bring to mind the experience of a particular child (who might even have been you) for whom life has provided many challenges. How might consideration of their spirituality be dismissed as non-essential 'icing on the cake'?
- How might their spirituality be seen as fundamental to their predicament?

To act upon . . .

List the things you do, or could do, to protect young children's spiritual capacities from being overshadowed as they grow older.

List the things that could damage or stunt young children's spiritual capabilities.

3 Encountering children's spirituality

Getting in touch with your childhood spirituality

In Chapter 1, we saw that it is not particularly helpful to think of adult and child spiritualities as totally separate. A lot is shared: children become adults for whom childhood spiritual experiences may have been hugely formative. And adults, in a spiritual sense, are striving to become childlike.

In trying to get to grips with the challenges of working alongside children's spirituality, it can be very helpful to look at your own spirituality, both now and as a child. It might be that we can only recognize what the spirituality of others (e.g. children) means when we begin to recognize it in ourselves. People who feel they work closely with children's spirituality report that this has a profound effect on their own spiritual life too.

Childhood memories

One way to become more attuned to what spirituality is like, especially the kind that includes children, is to make an inventory of some of the lasting impressions from your own childhood experience.

What were you *really* like as a child? Once we are grown up, childhood can become a bit generalized in our minds. We may talk about 'children' as though they are all rather alike, for instance, we may make general comparisons between children today and in the past. (Have attention spans changed? Is playfulness different because of computers?) Or we may be tempted to pigeonhole children because of what we know about their age or gender, for instance, making general assumptions about 'most three-year-olds' or 'most eight-year-old boys'. While general knowledge about childhood development can be helpful, we can lose touch with what it really felt like to be a particular child, especially the complexity or strength of what we felt about being 'me'.

The child who was you

A good way to reconnect with your childhood is to think back to a really special toy, game or pastime. It might have been racing matchbox cars, dressing dolls, playing schools, making dens, reading or chatting with your teddy. Maybe it was riding your bike along a particular route or perhaps you had an imaginary world or liked playing an instrument. Did you have a dangerous game or activity, something your parents did not know you got up to? Whatever it was, try to recall how it made you feel. Why was it so enjoyable? Do you still like playing that way now in some sense?

Think and discuss . . .

- What was your favourite toy/game/way of spending time?
- How did this make you feel?

Often our favourite toy or game gave us a sense of being really alive or at least switched on in a way we did not feel at other times. It may have given us a 'language' for things, a way of thinking things through, mostly without depending on words. At the same time, there was perhaps nothing very deliberate or conscious in our pursuit of this enjoyable activity. While mattering intensely, probably it just evolved naturally.

So when you next look at a child in your church, wonder about their capacity to feel really switched on, to make meaning without words and do things that really matter to them.

Your memories of 'something sacred'

Another way to form an impression of what 'childhood spirituality' means is by recalling moments, places or activities that gave you a sense of 'something sacred', even if you didn't have words to identify it in that way. Don't feel restricted to church or explicitly religious connections. This exercise is as important for those who didn't go to church or experience religious belief as for those who did.

Often the first thing people say when asked to do this is, 'I've never thought about that before', and so it's not easy to find memories quickly, though they may be quite vivid when they come. Take time, perhaps turning the question into a conversation with a friend.

Think and discuss . . .

- A 'sense of the sacred' when I was a child was about . . .

Almost no one doing this exercise recalls the specific content of a church experience, a 'lesson' or particular prayer. As we choose how to expend our energies in nurturing children's spiritual lives today, it may be very important to accept that the content of our efforts is much less significant than we had thought.

Things adults commonly *do* identify as the spiritual in their childhood include: nature, light, the atmosphere in a particular place, music, ritual, the qualities of a particular person, secret or private time (e.g. alone in bed or in your den) or being caught up in a very large gathering.

What we can learn about spirituality from this remembering exercise is *how clear the feel of things can be* – for example, a sense of peace, of mystery or fear, of belonging or a sense of the transcendent. Sometimes, years later, people can recapture that feeling just by thinking about it. Having the right words for this sense did not matter; clarity is not just about words.

For a lot of people, *the validity of the experience* is startling. As an adult, there may be lots of ways in which the particular context and content of the memory could be reinterpreted. For example, for some people a death may have represented a particular period of awareness of the sacred. The memory may be about feeling confused about why you went to church to say goodbye to a box in which the dead person was meant to be, or about feeling weird every time you used the paint set the deceased once gave you. Being able now, as an adult, to fill in what was missing from your understanding at the time neither invalidates (nor improves on the validity) of that original sense. At some important level, it still feels just as valid as it ever was.

Often we never shared these kinds of experiences with others, or even considered doing so. There are some practical reasons for that, such as our parents seeming too busy or not interested in that kind of thing, or these thoughts tended to come when we were alone anyway. However, the privacy of spiritual experiences is something to learn from too. It might have felt invasive to have our spirituality analysed, or we didn't want someone else's meaning and words stretched over our own. For adults, it is very important to take a 'go gently' approach, following the child's lead rather than our own agenda.

Think and discuss . . .

- 'Adult only' elements of spirituality – what is important to your spiritual life now that could not have been possible when you were a child?
- Given what seemed spiritual to you as a child, what could have helped you open up more to this? Could the church have played a positive role?

Getting in touch with children's spirituality
(How it feels to them – how it sounds to us)

In most of our encounters with children, as parents, teachers and so on, our primary focus is not on their spiritual characteristics. But research studies that have deliberately focused on children's spirituality give us important clues on what to notice. From these we can also gather tips about how to be supportive of children's often active and complex spiritual lives. And we can pick up ideas about how to encourage spiritual exploration through conversation – how to hear what's really being said, and how to provide opportunities for children to say more.

Talking about spirituality – the tip of the iceberg

Most studies of children's spirituality have been restricted to what children can talk about. Simply to become sensitive enough to hear how much children have to say is a worthwhile goal, and gives us more than enough pointers for children's ministry.

In most situations, adults find it hard to inhibit the urge to talk in favour of listening to children. And this sends discouraging signals so that when we do ask for the children's contribution, they can feel so conscious of their inability to express themselves with the authority the adult has modelled that they are unable to speak freely. In effect, all our talking may be 'teaching' them that they can't speak about spiritual things, and that to do so requires expert knowledge and fluency. And yet, when given free rein, children can talk at length, and in depth, about most spiritual issues, including the purpose of life, the mystery of death, their experience of God, the question of suffering and the reality of evil. Obviously they do this in their own way, and listening requires a generous ear to recognize these themes, and willingness to give the time needed to follow their sometimes chaotic train of thought.

Verbal expression, however, probably represents just the tip of the iceberg. Non-verbal spiritual expressions and responses are at least as important, not just for younger, less verbal children, but also for those with fluent enough language.

In valuing what children can have to say about spiritual life, we need to be very careful that they do not infer that a verbal approach is the only way to spiritual perception. The wrong kind of focus on spiritual talk might indirectly teach children to dismiss the powerful ways in which insight comes to us non-verbally. Chapter 4 suggests some ways of paying attention to the non-verbal channels in spirituality.

Getting started

Children can be very sensitive to the social demands of communication – what they think we want them to say. They can sense they lack the skill to 'wrap things up' and express honestly what they really think without hurting our feelings or getting into trouble. In contexts where children perceive strong cues about 'what you want us to say or think', as at church or about churchy things, it can be hard to encourage frank conversations. There is, of course, the often quoted story of the Sunday school teacher who asked the children to guess what she was thinking of based on clues such as, 'It has a bushy tail; it likes nuts', and received the reply, 'Well, it sounds like a squirrel but I know you must mean Jesus.'

So, conversations with children about their spiritual thoughts and feelings are not simply a matter of asking the right questions. Adults need to become alert to whether the children's comments are genuine and heartfelt or are merely obliging the demands of the context. This may mean giving unnatural value and attention to 'off-the-wall' or out-of-turn comments and reactions that leak out in more churchy contexts – such as when a child expresses horror on hearing the words 'this is my blood' during the Communion service or wants to discuss a seemingly tangential thread in a Bible story.

It can also mean accepting that, for children, church-based contexts may be the *least* conducive to spiritual conversations.[6] Conversations in the car, the bath, at bedtime or just when you are least prepared for them, are often much more important. Moreover, all who are involved in these moments (the child, the parent, the carer, the siblings) deserve to be supported to recognize the validity of these moments of spiritual engagement.

Candid comments

The following quotes came from children speaking 'off the record' to an adult, not in or from their church context. When able to speak openly like this, a lot of children reveal that they are left cold by conventional spirituality or situations that are *meant* to support spiritual life.

Praying	*It just feels like you are doing something for your religion.*
	(boy aged ten)

In a mosque	*You have to pray or just wait for your parents.*
	(girl aged six)

Collective worship	*It's just a waste of time. I'd rather be working.*
	(girl aged ten)

Sunday school

It's so boring, I somehow never want to go, singing and talking is all it is.

(girl aged six)

But children associate a much wider range of feelings with *their* spirituality. For some it feels wishful, like imagining, but genuinely comforting:

Looking at the sky

I think about Jesus and things, and I think about little tiny stories about stars. And I think about the song Twinkle twinkle little star, and sometimes I sing it . . . well I imagine little tiny stories in my head . . . and once there was a time I imagined it . . .

(Interviewer

Can you remember that?)

It was about when I went to the moon and I saw a star and I went on it and I saw God under the sky . . . over the sky . . . it was really nice . . . sort of really nice and calm and things.

(girl aged six)

For some the predominant mood is uncertainty, a sense of searching:

On the mystery of creation/the universe

No one has an answer, because no one knows . . . someday I'll discover like another part of life, like a jigsaw, like you've got all the pieces apart from one and then you just find it.

(boy aged ten)

For some the feeling is the 'logic' of having a conscious religious standpoint, the feeling of making and referring to an explanatory system – a personal theology:

On God

God created the earth for people to live and think the meaning of good . . . how he created the earth. I mean if God wasn't around with us, we wouldn't be alive. God wouldn't be around as well . . . There'd be

> *nothing . . . all around us . . . no space . . . no*
> *everything. . . SO we have to thank God for what*
> *he's given us. Because no space, no words, no*
> *computer, no anything. It'd just be nothing, just air,*
> *floating around. No God. If God wasn't around, we*
> *wouldn't be around. So I think, my view of God is*
> *uh . . . space . . . because space is black . . . and*
> *I can prove that God's black . . . He is space.*

(boy aged six)

For some a spiritual experience feels vivid and real, an encounter in everyday life, though it is increasingly relegated to the interior life if others don't take it as seriously:

> *Once in the night I saw this bishopy kind of alien.*
> *I said 'How are you' and he said I am the Holy*
> *Spirit . . . and I did think he was the Holy Spirit.*

(Interviewer   What did you feel like . . . were you shocked?)

> *I was going to say that, yeah, So I called my mum*
> *and dad, and they knew that the holy spirit was a*
> *ball of fire. He wasn't a ball of fire, so they said*
> *'Go on, go on, off with you!*

(Interviewer   So they didn't think it was the Holy Spirit?)

> *No*

(Interviewer   What do you think? Do you think they were right or
do you think they were mistaken?)

> *Er . . . they were right . . . yeah . . . But I often felt*
> *the holy spirit in me . . . once when I was alone and*
> *running down the High Street I heard Him say, 'Did*
> *I mind that the holy spirit knew me?' And that was*
> *the day I became a Christian.*

(boy aged six)

For some it feels ominous and better avoided:

Asked about mystery   *Um, looking outside my house when it's dark night time, that's really a mystery . . . um it's like still and horrible and I don't really like it.*

(boy aged six)

For some it feels overwhelmingly beautiful and refreshing:

A sense of heaven   *a mist of perfume, with gold walls, and rainbow stretched over God's throne and . . . a transparent mist . . . like I can't explain it, like a smell, a real cloud of smell, a lovely smell, like when you wake up on a dull winter morning and then when you go to sleep and wake up the birds are chirping, the last drops of snow are melting away and the treetops, shimmering in the breeze, and it's a spring morning . . . but I suppose it is a season at all, not really, because it [heaven] is just a day in delight every day.*

(girl aged six)

quotes from Rebecca Nye's research with David Hay, *The Spirit of the Child*[7]

Think and discuss . . .

═══

If possible, find a partner and compare notes about what you each hear in these quotes.

● What impression do you form of each child?

● How you could encourage the conversation to go on?

═══

How to hear and how to respond?

It's not easy for adults to hear the feelings that can represent the child's spiritual approach. The adult ear tends to be distracted by the content of what the children say or do. Sometimes our very 'understanding' of childhood (developmental theory, educational theory, etc.) gets in the way of opportunities to learn about childhood's spiritual aspects. For example, we might focus on the child's expression being too literal when he is trying to explore an abstract idea (like the boy above who ends up saying that God is black in an attempt to speak about his sense of God in everything and the antithesis of nothingness). Or our ears can hear mostly a rambling description that we dismiss as 'just typical of a chatty child thinking as she speaks', and we miss the profound insight it produces (like the girl above who describes heaven as 'a day in delight everyday').

Tip: focus on feeling

Attending to feelings rather than content is a good rule of thumb. Indeed, perhaps adults are misled by their apparent capacity to adopt clearer, so-called more 'legitimate' forms and content for their spirituality (religion, psychological language, the arts). In the process of adopting these forms, an adult may lose sight of the significant, inspiring feeling that can instigate and perpetuate spiritual attention. Children, by contrast, are closer to the feelings, and often have only a tenuous handle on the content.

An analogy with learning to speak in a foreign language may help us to appreciate the difficulty. In a sense, in talking about their spiritual life, children are attempting to translate what they know into a second language, sometimes non-verbal knowing to verbal language or 'my language for this' into 'Christian language for this'. It can be very disheartening if the listener pays more attention to correcting grammar than to the meaning and feeling behind the words, especially if what the speaker is trying to talk about really matters to them. It could be like phoning the emergency services when we are in a foreign country to report a matter of life and death importance, and having the operator correcting our choice of words or syntax! So if a child uses unorthodox or even 'incorrect' content from a Christian adult perspective (the Holy Spirit is a 'bishopy alien'), the key thing is the feeling and the intention behind what is said, not its accuracy. (In any case, of course, the Holy Spirit may indeed be a bishopy alien and much more.)

Tip: look out for signs of individuality

Another signal that can alert us to times when children are genuinely speaking from the heart, in their 'spiritual voice', is when they choose to draw on material or topics that are especially salient to them. Possibly each of us has a distinctively personal signature, that is, a style or area of interest through which the things that 'really matter' most naturally find a voice. For one child it might be in vivid stories about a fantasy landscape, for another it might be in an earnest debating style. There are children who seem unduly aware of the physical qualities of experience, and there are others who are easily inspired by the aesthetic character of things.

Sometimes you can actually hear the contrast between the voice (in tone, choice of words, flow or posture) that children use when talking about conventional spiritual matters, such as their attitudes to church and prayer (ordinary voice), and what feels spiritual to them in particular ('signature voice'). Discovering a child's authentic voice and personal signature clearly depends on making the effort to know each child well, and encouraging them to draw from this source as valuable. You might spot this voice in the area of an activity they really love – the theme they often draw, the toy or pastime they adore, the topic they always bring up or their role in the group (questioner, clown, helper, silent observer).

Clearly, a goal for spiritual nurture is for children to realize that their particular way of approaching spiritual matters is valid for Christian spirituality too. In other words, being authentic in our relationship with God is a much greater value than being conformist.

As so much of children's work takes place in groups, knowing and supporting the individuality of each child is complicated. It challenges us to accept that prayer, Bible study, mission and so on are not to be reduced to a 'one-size-ought-to-fit-all-children' policy. Instead, rather like buying children's shoes, we may need to offer different sizes and styles to suit each child's spiritual shape, even if this approach costs more.

Think and discuss . . .

- Think of a child you know really well. When and how is that child most authentically herself or himself?
- What would be the 'costs' of adapting your group work with children to take individual spiritual styles into account? What would help you to find out more about each child's style?

Where religious language fits in – not easily

Churches have the difficult task of helping children discover that religious language is a worthwhile way to express spirituality. Having spiritual experiences and ideas is not at all dependent on having church language or church experience. Children usually have their own natural sense of God, with or without a name for that. Ana-Maria Rizzuto puts it like this, 'No child arrives at the house of God without his pet God under his arm.'[8] However, a repeated research finding is that many children feel unable to share this kind of personal spirituality with anyone, least of all those in the church.[9] They too easily think they are quite alone in having such feelings and thoughts. They don't realize that these have any value, and before long begin to feel embarrassed and dismissive about them. As they come into contact with Christian language during their school years, they seem to 'learn' that Christian language is *not* spiritually useful. (Rather that it is a language of morals, history and good examples.) Certainly some children use bits and pieces of it in expressing their spirituality, but the way adults use it seems to give no clue that it's about spiritual life as they know it and feel it.

Children may find it especially hard when religious language bumps into their natural sense of the sacred. Trying to help them become users of Christian vocabulary (both verbal and non-verbal) might inadvertently suggest that their own natural language and prior experiences are suspect or even invalid. There is a danger that in teaching children to use the 'right' language, we imply that they must discard the powerful, personal experiences and ideas they already have in favour of images borrowed from our tradition, which may seem pale by comparison, at least initially.

A good approach is to invite children simply to enter directly into religious language, to be engaged by it and get absorbed by it. This is different from trying to persuade or convince them that it is 'saying something' and 'translating' what that is for them. We often tell a Bible story, but rather than trusting God's word to speak for itself in God's own way, we rush to explain what it says to *us*. We miss the chance to explore how it can make meaning for the child.

This is about offering opportunities for religious language to be occasions when children experience ways God is with them and they can be with God, rather than suggesting that *if* they learn to 'speak religious', *then* their relationship with God can begin. Worship, Bible stories and prayer can be offered as opportunities or spaces for children to find quite natural ways to be themselves, and to be with God, and to enjoy their own native languages of play and story. This can mean all sorts of things, including the freedom simply to enjoy the stories for their own sake, allowing their archetypal themes of freedom, loss, love, identity and so on to resonate intuitively, playfully, often without words, with the children's sense of these themes in their own lives.

Spiritual life is more than just the odd special moment

Over the years, research has found that it pays to use a wide net to catch the great variety of forms taken by children's spirituality. It is not enough to be restricted to special experiences that children might be able to talk about, such as a moment when they felt close to or more aware of God. Conversations can also explore children's imaginings, ideas, feelings and ways of relating in order to develop a broader impression of their spiritual life. Casting the net wide also conveys to children the important message that there are many valid ways of searching for spiritual truth. Learning this at an early stage could make all the difference later on when children might make decisions about whether faith is too narrow and exclusive for them.

Some children can share definitive experiences, like the little boy quoted above who spoke of his vision of the Holy Spirit as a bishopy alien (see p. 00). Others might be keen to talk about what imagined spiritual experiences, such as encountering angels, could be like. Many relish the chance to discuss spiritual ideas, such as their view of mystery or death. Feelings can be just as important a means of expression, as when, in response to the joy of Christmas Day, a five-year-old girl draws a graphic picture of the sorrow of the crucifixion, possibly expressing her spiritual need for complexity and balance.

As adults, we can develop 'wider net casting' skills by looking at *every* activity in terms of its spiritual qualities, not just conversations that clearly mark themselves out in that way. Train your skills by observing a normal conversation, argument or 'normal' period of activity through a spiritual lens – a chat in the bath, for instance, or a trip to the park with friends. Then ask: What does this reveal about a child's ways of being with God or God being with them?

A different kind of knowing

Something familiar to researchers is how erratic children can be in exposing their spiritual life to others. One day they may be full of it, next time seemingly indifferent. This may be not so different from the spiritual lives of adults but we hide it better when there's not much going on! In terms of children's ministry, this is a reminder that spiritual knowing is more slippery than other kinds of knowledge or understanding. Children who know a lot about football, always do; children who are secure in their knowledge of the alphabet rarely lose that knowledge.

Working around the erratic ways in which children express their spiritual life means valuing who they are now, not what they said last time. It also means being honest with them and saying that people don't always feel ready to do this kind of work, so that children don't feel negatively judged by you, and they don't set themselves unrealistically high expectations.

Think and discuss . . .

Studies of spiritual experience suggest that in childhood there is a sense of clarity, validity and a directly personal quality.

- What implications does this have for debates about children receiving Holy Communion?
- What implications does this have for other aspects of church life where attendance is restricted on age grounds?

Joanna's garden

In conversation, ten-year-old Joanna spoke about lacking confidence in herself, and about her fears about death and nothingness. But speaking about her imaginary garden, Joanna said she liked to play at being the Queen of this garden in which she enjoyed magnanimous power to bring things back to life. In her imaginary garden it was always sunny and peaceful. She explained that her garden was a retreat when her noisy, and sometimes gloomy, home life got on top of her. She was aware that going to her garden was helpful, and sensed that for her this kind of thing had transforming potential.

> It's a really nice garden if you're lonely or you haven't got anything to do . . . you just close your eyes, lie down and it comes into a nice little garden and . . . if everyone stopped and thought about what they were doing, you might actually have a better life . . . because people might understand you a little better . . . So I think if life is a little brighter you see brighter things.

But seeking solitude was not completely satisfactory. She was acutely aware of loneliness too.

> Sometimes I feel very lonely when I am alone with God because I can't see God and I can't hear God, I just think about God. I feel really lonely, so I like being with people sometimes but sometimes I am pretty glad to be alone, if I've got someone bugging me like my sisters.

- What spiritual needs are glimpsed here?
- What opportunities are there for the role of the church in Jo's life?
- Can you imagine ways in which the church could inadvertently threaten Jo's spirituality?
- Does Jo's spirituality have something to offer the life of your church /group?

Wondering

Godly Play is a highly sophisticated approach to Christian spiritual nurture.[10] Godly Play's careful techniques of facilitating spiritual conversation model and encourage what is called 'wondering'. The art of wondering suggests good practices that can be applied in a wide range of encounters with children, not only in Godly Play sessions.

The adult adopts an open style – wondering rather than explaining. For example, 'I wonder what you liked in this story. I wonder what the most important part of this story is.' This invites children to enter into a freer thinking space, where the depth and breadth of the spiritual universe may be far larger than even the adult appreciated. The goal is to help the children explore what they think and feel, not to arrive at the conclusion the adult planned in advance. The end point is not set – the spirit can really move in mysterious ways!

Wondering is not primarily a roundabout way of asking the children to provide answers. Rather, it is used to help the children form the habit of wondering. This approaches spiritual expression and meaning-making as valuable processes, not merely means to an end. Habitually wondering about spiritual matters, and in response to spiritual content (such as Bible stories), inspires children to value the possibility that fresh insights might be yielded each time, as opposed to things being fixed once and for all. So a Godly Play style inspires adults to give special attention to the times when children do *not* respond to the wondering questions posed, but find inspiration in this 'wondering mode' to pose their *own*, different, wondering questions, even if those are quite 'off the wall'!

Wondering, in Godly Play sessions, makes a conscious effort to value all contributions, even those that are apparently silly, incoherent or shocking. This shifts the focus from listening preferentially to 'the expert' or to 'the answers'. Instead, by learning to hear from everyone, even from those whose contributions may seem totally 'other' or alien to our way of thinking, children are encouraged to develop more sensitive spiritual listening skills, which include attending to things heard inwardly or in other unconventional ways. Having a facilitator who accepts whatever they say is also likely to encourage children to feel safe to say more, and to risk saying things that are really hard to express, which is often the nature of deep spiritual material.

The skill of supporting spiritually rich conversation is therefore much less about carefully weaving the conversation through planned points to arrive at a conclusion, as a conventional teacher does, than about letting go and following the energy of the moment, where the spirit leads – which is often deeper, and nearly always the piece of work that needed to be done. For instance, even though a 'fun activity' was planned to follow up the discussion starter, the adult recognized the need to ditch that when the group felt moved (and safe enough) to discuss something dark or painful.

Think and discuss . . .

- I wonder what you like most about spiritual conversations with children (in your experience or in the examples given here)?
- I wonder what is most important about spiritual conversations with children?
- I wonder where you are, or could be, in helping children to talk about their spiritual lives?

This chapter has explored two ways we can help ourselves to get in touch with children's spirituality and, through that, help children share their spirituality with us. This is the crucial basis on which religious nurture can build, and with which it needs constantly to touch base. The next chapters focus on how we can learn to make our practice spirituality centred.

Summary: tips for encountering children's spirituality

- Recall your own experiences of being a child.
- Say less, hear more.
- Remember: it's not only about words.
- Be alert to child's views of convention, context and expectation.
- Value and enjoy the unusual and the spontaneous.
- Focus on feeling more than content.

- Listen for individual voice, spiritual signature.
- Avoid suggesting religious language is better than natural expression.
- Erratic is OK.
- Encourage wondering and questioning; limit explanation and answering.

4 Nurturing children's spirituality 1: some general principles

It cannot be emphasized too strongly that to do justice to the challenge of spirituality, we have to attend to more than simply what is said, to more than words. We need a guide to seeing, feeling and evaluating our practices and settings for their spiritual quality.

Six criteria for ensuring spiritual foundations

This chapter offers six criteria that lie at the core of achieving a 'best practice' policy for spirituality in day-to-day children's work. The idea is that in every situation you could use these criteria as a checklist to help take stock of how well children's spirituality is being supported. In one sense this is another way of 'defining' what spirituality entails, especially when that includes children. It is meant, however, to be a definition to really work with, a tool to evaluate and draw out best practice.

All the criteria are equally important, but for ease of recall they are set out as an acrostic. This might help you to get into a habit of 'auditing' each one of these areas. These are *general criteria* for best practice in supporting children's spirituality, so they can apply to all kinds of work with children – Sunday school, holiday clubs, all-age worship, collective worship in school, prayer, Christian nurture in the home and much more.

S pace

P rocess

I magination

R elationship

I ntimacy

T rust

S.P.I.R.I.T.

Space

Where we are can have a positive or negative influence on our spiritual well-being. Many Christians have a strong attachment to a particular familiar place that especially helps them enter into God's presence – perhaps a church, a place of pilgrimage or corner of their home. This special place becomes a 'sanctuary' – our experiences here convincing us that this is both a holy, and safe, place to be.

Physical space

The selection and positioning of things for this space, their beauty or simplicity, often add to this experience. Sacred spaces can speak their own language of meaning and help us express what we value, which can be both personal and powerful. Some changes to the space can disturb us, and reveal the degree to which the space feeds our need for spiritual equilibrium (e.g. a new seating arrangement in worship). Other changes might be exciting, helping to keep our spiritual life dynamic and connected to the changes outside the space (e.g. marking the different Church seasons by changing colours).

Children are especially sensitive to the feel of a place, even as they cross the threshold. They can 'read' its language easily. A village hall might say, 'run, shout (there's a great echo!) or do what you like'. A meeting room with tables, chairs and posters with words might say to them, 'school, knowledge, being clever or feeling dumb'. A place that looks like a toy room might say, 'rummage in the toy boxes, kill some time till Mum's finished' or, 'not long till I'm too old for all this'.

Often in our churches work with children takes place in spaces that *don't* easily lend themselves to a sense of 'God is here', 'this is a holy and safe place to be yourself'; or the things in the space don't help children make meaningful discoveries using Christian language.

In the 'proper church' spiritual value and meaning are usually deliberatively supported: for example, by a permanently visible empty cross, an accessible communion table or reserved seating for wheelchair users. Why do we make an effort to make the 'proper' church space the best it can be? Why does it matter to have it clean, organized (things can't be left just anywhere), with an eye to decoration (flowers, colours)? Why do church councils take time over choosing new religious art and artefacts? We do these things because, indirectly, they express our theology, our understanding of God's nature and our desire to relate to that. We're avoiding being *careless* – and this says we think that God is worth caring about.

By contrast, spaces used in our work with children can actually undermine the spiritual meaning our words and activities are trying to share with them. Perhaps the focal point of the space in which they meet is the wastepaper basket or fire extinguisher. Maybe the carpet is dirty or it's the one the main church decided was too tatty so passed on. Often the resources are random donations of old toys and Christian books and the images or art on the walls include things the church just hasn't got around to letting go of. The quality of lighting and heating may be problematic too. This all conveys a careless mindset, a 'none of this really matters' attitude, a message about being second-rate. It sends a negative message about how children are valued by God and in this place. It can say, 'God's ways of being with children and children's ways of being with God are not worth carefully investing in, we'll just muddle through.'

Reflect on the spiritual principles at work in the main building of your church, and you'll find the clues to guide you in creating a helpful kind of space for the children too to do their spiritual work.

Also, ask the children to describe, draw or construct the conditions that convey a sense of the sacred to them. You might invite them to think about a place they've been to where they felt 'God is here' and explore with them the features of that place that they were aware of. You can also ask them to think of places where it's really hard to feel 'God is here'. What is it about those places that makes it difficult to have a sense of God?

Some things you cannot easily change and very few of us work in ideal spaces where every detail has been carefully chosen, designed and maintained (which is the goal in a Godly Play room).[11] But just making an effort with the space will say something in itself. For example:

● If you meet in a big draughty hall, but for your church and children sacred space is preferably somewhere intimate and in the round, you could section off one part of the hall with a screen or chairs and find a soft rug to sit on together.

- Creating a clear 'threshold' can make a huge difference to a sense of sacred space – that sense of 'coming in' and 'coming out', of welcome and being sent forth. Children have good imaginations, so even an artificial threshold – a strip of material to cross over, a row of chairs or screens with a gap for entering – can help to mark the space as set apart.

- If a shared room is often left untidy or in need of cleaning when it's the children's time to use it, invite the children to volunteer as helpers who come early and help prepare the room. This conveys a strong message to all (even the wider congregation ideally) about the worth of what happens in this space, and *who* it happens with – the children, the children's work leaders and God.

- If the space for the children and the 'church' space feel entirely unrelated (e.g. one is a Portakabin, the other a twelfth-century cathedral!), a connection can be made by placing something from each in the other space, such as carrying a cross or Bible from the church to the children's room, and placing the children's offering or children's Bible on the altar.

Think and discuss . . .

Think of different spaces/places where you (as an adult) have worshipped or met with a Christian group.

- What negatively affects your spiritual engagement (e.g. seating arrangements, the way in, the likelihood of extraneous noise or interruptions, visual irritations)?

Emotional space

But this is not only about auditing physical space. Emotional space matters too. This requires careful thought both about how to manage the space we give to one another and how to help the children learn to give space to each other.

Emotional space includes the space to be somewhat apart, to be ourselves and perhaps have different opinions, but also the space in which we can feel closely held and safe. This dual challenge is at the core of creating and safeguarding any spiritual community – our local church, our ecumenical relationships, our families. This is also part of our experience (and children's experience) of God – times of feeling close and held, and times of feeling farther away, the immanence and transcendence of God. The point is to ensure that *both* kinds of emotional space are offered. Learning good habits in this area cannot start too early, as this is frequently an area in which Christian communities fracture.

Auditory space

Finally, you can inspect the auditory space to see how this supports children's spiritual needs.

The previous chapter gave a number of tips about encouraging spiritual conversations with children, and referred to the 'talk less, listen more' principle. This is about creating safe space too, for example, habitually leaving longer gaps after a child has spoken in case they have more to say and allowing time for everyone to take in and value their contribution. Or internally counting to at least seven if no one responds to an open question – considerable reflection may be required before a reply can be formed and when that process is interrupted with another question, children are discouraged from engaging deeply. Instead of prematurely intruding into the auditory space when children have been speaking or planning to speak, adults can simply show their response and interest through facial expressions and 'mmms'.

Being sensitive to auditory space is also about taking *silence* seriously. Children who choose not to speak are not spaces where 'nothing' is happening. Silence can be a way of saying something so important that it can't be put into words.

Think and discuss . . .

Stand at the threshold of a space where you meet with children (your Sunday school room/where you say family prayers/ the holiday club venue): find at least a dozen adjectives to describe this physical space. Then sit where a child would normally sit in that space: add more descriptors to your list.

● Do you think of God as being like any of the things on your list?

● Do you think of children as being like any of the things on your list?

● What would you most like to change to make this space a better space for children to be with God and God to be with children?

Think and discuss . . .

Try leaving a seven-second 'space' next time you are with children, for example, when telling a story, after asking a question/hearing responses, or when they show you something they've drawn.

● What do you predict will happen?

● What really happens?

S.**P**.I.R.I.T.

Process

Spirituality is more about process than product. When production is emphasized, spirituality can get squeezed out. Production suggests that the end result is all important, and that this kind of work can be 'finished', freeing us up to do something else. But spiritual life is an on-going piece of work, not something to be completed or get prizes for. Prayer and worship are spiritual processes, not ends in themselves. Process honours the present moment too, and learning to be fully present. Similarly, childhood deserves to be treated as a process rather than a production line for delivering adults, or Christians.

Children especially need help to value the often quiet, slow, iterative qualities of 'processing' since so much else in their lives does not. We can help by checking where our emphasis lies in teaching, in the activities we plan and in the ways we celebrate the children's gifts and their sense of who they really are.

Valuing spiritual processing in teaching can mean being less concerned with getting to a fixed learning 'outcome' (teaching 'product') and more with enjoying the fresh thoughts and feelings the material stimulates.

Sometimes our approach to teaching with children *pretends* to value process, for example, asking children open-ended questions such as, 'Who is your favourite superhero?' or, 'How did Jesus feel when he was baptized?' Yet often this is a disguise for pushing forward the teacher's agenda, which has a fixed end point and knowledge product to be 'fished out' in a roundabout way. The children interpret this 'process' as merely a game – the game of 'guess what the teacher really wants us to say' (to which the right answer is nearly always 'Jesus'). They learn to associate biblical material and its potential to make meaning in their lives with a pseudo-reflective process. And they learn that the final explanation is valued much more than the ongoing, hopefully lifelong, engagement with the journey towards understanding.

There needs to be an eye to safeguarding the spiritual process in art and craft activities. Ideally these are chances to invite children to work creatively, reflectively, with Christian language, to make meaning. The prayerful quality that these activities can have is best conveyed by ensuring that the children have sufficient, uninterrupted time to become absorbed in the process of being creative. We are not very good at that, and even assume that children need constant supervision, 'bite-sized' time frames, and that the creative work only 'counts' if we can get the child to talk about it. Rushing to finish one task after another (e.g. first do the word search, now make a whale, then contribute to the group banner) tends to promote a product-centred mindset that is antithetical to deep processing in spiritual life. It is also rather stressful rather than peace-giving.

Another way to give positive emphasis to process and, implicitly, to spirituality, is to limit the impression that 'products' and 'producers' get all the rewards. This is all too easily implied in 'show and tell' times, especially when accompanied by applause for what the children have done or achieved. Many adults perceive this as a way to demonstrate that they are a 'child-friendly' church, but when used too routinely 'show and tell' may not help children appreciate the value of process (the mistakes, the experiments, the times of incubation or contemplation) in their spiritual work.

Displaying pictures (usually only the 'finished ones') also puts more value on what the children can *do* than on who they are called to be. Again, balancing being child-friendly and child-*spirituality*-friendly is tricky. A good practical way around this issue is to be clear with the children about when they are working on something to be 'produced' for a purpose, such as to display or show others, and when they are not – that is, when their response will not be judged. The difference in mindset between these is similar to being asked as an adult to write some prayers to use in worship against being given space for your own prayer time in response to the sermon.

Think and discuss . . .

- What could be described as 'product focused' in your children's work?
- In what ways is process valued over product in your children's work?
- How could you help children value process in themselves and others even more than they do?

S.P.I.R.I.T.

Imagination

Spirituality depends on our being open and willing to go deeper. Imagination and creativity can resource this, but often very clear permission has to be given this is 'okay'. Many children and adults worry because they feel there must be right answers and correct explanations, as if spiritual language were like mathematics. But as Jerome Berryman points out, in Christian language the 'maths' approach gets nowhere near the mystery that is implied:

God the Father + God the Son + God the Holy Spirit = 1 not 3! (but 3 *in* 1?!)

Sometimes Christians are wary of the role of imagination and pass that message on to children in indirect ways. There's a fear that using imagination in the service of religious work is the same as suggesting that our beliefs in themselves are imaginary. But, as centuries of Christian art, literature and drama demonstrate, the religious imagination can be a wonderfully powerful tool for going deeper into our tradition and for strengthening our beliefs. It may often be more powerful, and more appropriate, than a non-imaginative style or language.

When Jesus was asked for spiritual information, such as, 'What is the kingdom of heaven?' or, 'Who is my neighbour?' he chose an imaginative style to convey the breadth and depth of these matters (i.e. parables: '[Imagine] it's like . . .'). He almost never gave a factual type of answer or explanation, but used his imagination and required his listeners to do the same. It's also interesting that though we try to declare our list of beliefs in the creed, for many, the highpoint in worship, when we come close to God, is Holy Communion. In that experience we imaginatively 'act out' or 'play through' our grasp of the mystery of Christ's body and blood being given and broken for us, like bread and wine to his disciples.

So children need every encouragement to get into the habit of using their imaginative faculties in the service of spiritual life. It is this that will help them both now, and in later years, to engage with the elements of religious practice. Encouraging real imagination will develop the spiritual skills they need as they sift through layers of meaning and make new discoveries.

Relatively simple additions to your practice can help signal that imagination is welcome, even needed here. For example:

- Include imaginative 'warm up' exercises, for example, 'How many different things could this prop be?!'

- Resist the urge to steer away from the apparently crazy comments or suggestions that children are bound to make sometimes! Pay serious attention to the off-the-wall suggestions, follow them up with the child and be surprised how often the most creative connections are made.

- Give opportunities for children to choose for themselves what to paint, draw or make in response to the input.

Luckily, children usually have highly agile imaginative faculties and this is another strength to build on rather than an obstacle to surmount. Compared to us, children are experts at imagining things 'completely differently' – the clothes peg can be a crocodile, the table with a sheet over it can be a castle. So in terms of fathoming the entirely different realities represented by 'kingdom values', 'the communion of saints' or 'the resurrection to eternal life', children can be at an advantage. In fact, we may need to pay particular attention to their imaginative takes on these things.

Checking the 'imagination' criteria in a spirituality audit of ministry with children needs to be done carefully. Sometimes adults are wonderfully imaginative in the ways they present Bible stories or spiritual realities to children, but this is not the same as enabling the children themselves to be imaginative and playful. In fact, the adult's creativity and imagination can sometimes leave little room for the child's! Often people feel unsuited to children's ministry because they can't come up with imaginative ideas and activities. Yet such people may actually have exactly what's called for: humility about imagination that will give priority to the children's own spiritual exploration and creativity.

Think and discuss . . .

- Where is imagination evident in your ministry with children? Rate each element or activity out of 5 – extremely imaginative (5) to extremely unimaginative (1).

- Compare with a colleague in the same setting – do you have the same understanding of imagination as a skill for spiritual life?

- When is imagination sometimes discouraged or suppressed?

- Who gets to hold the creative and imaginative reins, the leaders or the children?

S.P.I.**R**.I.T.

Relationship

Offering authentic models of relating to one another is right at the core of spirituality, especially for Christians. Although it can sometimes seem quite a private matter, spirituality is always an urge to relate and to connect. This does not mean that everyone needs to be in 'full-on spiritual relationships' with everyone else, since the primary relationship is between the individual and God. However, the overall quality of the relationships we experience, including through church experiences, can set parameters for how we relate spiritually.

What features of our relationships could help here? One might be to treat each person's spiritual perspective as valuable, regardless of age or knowledge. There can be a powerful effect on children in a mixed age group if the older or more knowledgeable (including the 'teacher') discover how to relate openly (not condescendingly) to different 'others'. This sharing and respect also helps promote a non-individualistic style of spiritual life – it's not just about me and my spiritual work, but how I am fed by, and can feed, other people's ways of working through things.

At a very practical level, you can be more proactive about developing a listening, respectful ethos. This includes modelling a way of responding to other people that shows that each person has value, rather than implying by our language ('that's the right answer') or other means (reward stickers, etc) that certain people, or certain kinds of contributions, are better than others. At school, usually because the teacher has to manage a large group, children learn to put up their hands to get a turn to speak. In practice, the result can be that they focus on planning what *they* are going to say, and not on listening to or being aware of others around them. A more relationship-sensitive, respectful habit can be to pass around a 'speaking' stone or holding cross to mark whose turn it is to contribute (and not to limit contributions to words, either).

Another feature might be to respect as 'holy ground' the space *between* individuals. Some see spirituality as the dynamic between people rather than a characteristic 'in' a person. This is an important challenge since it prioritizes our relationships – so the 'real' spiritual work is how we treat one another, not the topic for the day.

Think and discuss . . .

Try to 'audit' what the 'ground between us' actually feels like (between the children, and between the adults and children) at various points in the work you do.

- When and how does that space become 'holy'?
- Can debate, conflict, sadness or tiredness exist in the spaces between you without it becoming a spirituality-free zone?
- Can your ways of relating help to model that spiritual life is far more than warm fuzzy feelings, but includes righteous indignation, despair, reluctance and so on?

S.P.I.R.I.T.

Intimacy

Much of spirituality is about a sense of 'coming closer' to things. Keeping things at a distance is an important skill too in many situations. For example, in complex emotional situations we take refuge from being 'too involved'; theories and concepts help us get a distance on the minutiae of experiences; and theology helps us sort out overall themes in a very different way from the intimate practices of prayer and worship. Nevertheless, spirituality thrives on intimacy, it seizes opportunities to come closer, delve deeper, take risks and pursue passions.

Creating and supporting intimacy can be done in many different ways. It's not inevitably about providing privacy, small groups or cosy spaces. Cathedrals, mountaintops and ocean cruises can confer a sense of spiritual intimacy too. The central factor is probably 'feeling safe', a feeling that it's okay to come closer, to surrender to something greater than my conceptual (distancing) handle on things. This 'safety' needs to be well guarded – spiritual life itself is not a gentle ride necessarily. Intimacy provides the conditions from which the ride begins and to which it can return.

When churches work with children, a number of factors threaten the possibility of intimacy ever building up. The children may not come regularly or may not see one another at other times, increasing their sense of anxiety. There may be quite a few leaders, possibly with different styles and expectations, which puts the children on edge, wondering what 'this' one will do. The children may fear that they will be judged on how much they know, or feel that their affective responses are not the right ones (e.g. they really *like* the bit with Pharaoh's armies), or they fear that the congregation will laugh at their 'cute' answer, like last time. Or they might feel scared by the uniform mood ('fun, fun, fun!' or being 'very good and very quiet') that can't contain how they feel and who they are.

All these anxieties raise children's 'distancing barriers' and make it difficult for any intimate spiritual engagement to take place. They may feel too vulnerable to risk opening up at all, regardless of the quality of the material or the good intentions and integrity of the leaders. Children may be learning that church, of all places, is *not* a good place for their most personal spiritual work.

Creating a sense of safe, intimate time and space is a long-term project with each group and each child – slowly achieved and quickly broken. We need to have a deliberate policy of building in safety and intimacy-guarding features. For example, establishing that it is not acceptable to hijack things children have said in the safety of their small group to share them with the wider congregation in sermons or even over coffee with their family, without their genuine permission. And some children will be deeply suspicious of this promise of intimacy, and before venturing to expose anything personally significant they will need to test how true this offer is – for example, by saying or doing something a bit unusual (or naughty) to see if they are pushed away.

Think and discuss . . .

- Where did you feel safe as a child?
- What conferred that sense? What threatened it?
- What were you able to be closer to as a result?
- How do you value and protect intimacy in your children's ministry?
- What threatens that intimacy?

S.P.I.R.I.**T**.

Trust

Spirituality involves trusting. In the first instance, trust is needed because spirituality does not usually deal in empirical evidence, visions or voices. Trust is comfortable with different kinds of knowing, and not knowing, evidenced by a strong tradition in spiritual literature.

Trust is also essential to the maintenance of spiritual life – trusting that there's still value when this life feels all dried up, baffling or more than we can take. This kind of trust encourages us not to run away or raise our barriers.

Trust implies taking a relaxed, perhaps longer-term view, of feedback and 'results'. It is connected to the emphasis on process over product that, as we have seen, is especially meaningful for understanding spirituality.

How might trust be generally evident in children's ministry practice? How is trust part of nurture in Christian homes? The idea is that when trust (or any of the other SPIRIT criteria) is deeply embedded in *our* attitudes and actions, the non-verbal language of spirituality will be clearly available for children to hear and adopt for themselves. In a culture of *mis*trust, however, children could find it difficult to distinguish spiritual sense from conflicting noise, and even mistakenly adopt the 'noise' as their language.

Trust is especially evident (or, if absent, mistrust becomes evident) in the view adults have of their own role. When that role tends towards being controlling, authoritative or personality driven, then trust is undermined. For instance, assuming too controlling a role (e.g. 'the *important* point you need to hear in this story is . . .') suggests a lack of trust in God to speak for himself. Assuming an authoritative role (e.g. not taking a child's feelings seriously: 'It's silly to feel sad, Easter is a *happy* time') implies a lack of trust in the child. And it can be dangerous to assume too personality-driven a role (e.g. a special persona/teddy/puppet that can 'translate' faith) in case the children interpret this as a slur on the ability of our faith stories and tradition to stand for themselves – a lack of trust in the strength of the tradition.

It may be helpful to ask three simple questions of your practice:

1. Is there room for greater *trust in God* in this process?
2. Is there room for greater *trust in the child* in your approach?
3. Is this approach signalling basic *trust in the faith* (the Bible, the liturgy, our doctrines)?

Some situations require us to be more consciously trusting. We may need to call on 'trust' reserves, but thinking of this as a way to enhance the spiritual character of our work should encourage us in such moments. For example, it is common in work with children to worry about being able to say 'the right thing'. If a child shares something painful ('my granny's going to die'), or something hurtful ('Sammy's idea of angels is really stupid'), be aware that you are not the only resource. Before jumping in with a nervous and hurried response of your own, trust that the other children may be able to help you say, or do, something helpful in response. Trust that God can help you, and the children, to discern a way through this: that this is not all down to you. Adopting this attitude will help to slow you down and convey a powerful sense of unflinching trust to the children.

Reviewing the S.P.I.R.I.T. checklist

Space, **P**rocess, **I**magination, **R**elationship, **I**ntimacy, **T**rust

This chapter has moved us on from thinking about the qualities of spirituality found in children, to considering the qualities of spirituality we can make provision for.

The S.P.I.R.I.T. checklist suggests six areas that affect the spiritual quality of work with children. By taking deliberate action to safeguard Space, Process, Imagination, Relationship, Intimacy and Trust we stand a better chance of providing the conditions in which children's spirituality can flourish.

Think and discuss . . .

Think about a particular context in which you support children (at home, in your Sunday school, in a holiday club or in leading all-age worship).

- In which of the six areas do you feel you are already doing quite a good job?
- In which of the six areas do you feel there is a long way to go?

Can you think of other contexts in which you could use the S.P.I.R.I.T. model to 'audit' how spirituality is valued and supported?

5 Nurturing children's spirituality 2: spiritual practices

Prayer

> Notice that not once did Jesus make his disciples pray. He just kept on praying until they could contain their hunger no longer and asked Him to teach them how to pray.
>
> Pat Lynch, *Awakening the Giant*

These words by Pat Lynch are about the good spiritual teacher who waits until the pupils are ready to listen, and not only to listen but also to hear. It may seem to make sense to follow this patient Christ-like approach, but in practice, with children, it is probably rare deliberately to wait for each child to make the first move. (Interestingly, with groups of adults exploring the Christian faith, current practice is usually to take a much more 'only if you'd like to' approach.)

Your reluctance to wait could be because you feel obliged by your role as children's work leader to teach children to pray whether or not they have asked for that. Even where children are not explicitly made to pray, they may be acutely sensitive to the demands of the situations we allow to exist that give them a sense of 'I have to' – for example, when children are set the homework of writing a prayer or find themselves visiting a church where, in the children's group, each child is asked to contribute during 'prayers', and so feels obliged to do the same.

Think and discuss . . .

- What happens if we *don't* wait for this moment and try to 'make' children pray?
- Does this ever benefit the child? Are the prayers ever 'better'?
- What is the danger if we *do* try to wait for that moment?

Praying for *children and for your work with them*

Waiting for children to ask about prayer doesn't put a block on praying. Children can be prayed *for,* whether or not they are present, and can be aware that they are being prayed for. This might happen before and after the children meet or whenever your team meets for planning. You might especially reflect prayerfully on individual children – the very quiet, shy child who you can't get a handle on at all or the really challenging child who you half hope won't come this time and disrupt your plans.

Sometimes we can go round and round in discussions about 'what to do' about this or that child. Setting this conversation in the context of prayer is not meant to sanitize it by excluding the irritations or hopelessness we may feel, as if we were seeing prayer as a quick fix way of getting God to make all the children seem lovely. But it can be helpful to ask: How is this child stretching the ways in which God is understood to be a presence in our work? Is there any way in which we can see the issues they present as 'God's way of being with them and their way of being with God'?

There might be a sense in which each different (and especially difficult) child provides an important aspect of God that we are prone to downplay, that is, a face of God that is in danger of being missed out of our spiritual perspective. For example, a child can symbolize God's power to disrupt the familiar and surprise us, or a chaotic child can challenge us to remember God's presence in the chaos of the beginning. Maybe also certain children, furious when promises aren't kept and people let them down, can provide us with the angry face of God, and yet others may be signals of God who is hidden, silent and can't ever be 'known'.

Just keep on praying until . . .

It is vital to provide conditions and experiences that make prayer the natural response – conditions that help children develop an appetite for prayer. A lot of that is being prayerful ourselves, modelling a spiritual way of being, as Jesus did. So this is not about modelling 'duty' so much as satisfying our hunger for God's presence. But, once again, this is not about only the verbal or the conventional ways we can pray. Children will be just as sensitive to non-verbal prayerfulness, perhaps more so. In particular, they will feel unsettled by the mixed messages they receive when verbal prayer is offered in a context that feels prayer-less. Older children will spot the hypocrisy of that very quickly and reject the authenticity of the person leading the prayer, and the very notion of prayer, prayer having become tainted, possibly for life.

In the previous chapter, six criteria for supporting spirituality were proposed: space, process, imagination, relationship, intimacy and trust. These can also guide how we approach prayer.

Space and prayer

Obviously prayer is not just about special times or places, but we can be sustained by the qualities of special time and place to develop the capacity to pray anywhere and despite any distraction. In a room or meeting hall that is rather high energy because of its decor, its usual function or its noise level, to create a sense of inner spiritual space for prayer can be hard. It's not impossible, just that more needs to be done to compensate for the difficulties that the physical space presents.

One way of compensating can be to pay particular attention to the way the people make up the space – a sense of sacred space can be created by forming a circle or holding hands or by respecting personal space boundaries. A sense of sacred space can also be signalled by a change in the posture, gesture or eye gaze of the person leading the prayer time. The classic school assembly prayer led by a teacher from a platform while keeping a controlling eye on the pupils, who inhabits exactly the same space and posture when going on to complain about running in the corridors and the success of the football team, is clearly to be avoided!

Process and prayer

Younger children can get rather tangled up by the notion of petitionary prayer. Too easily this lends itself to the idea that this type of prayer is like a wish list for getting what they want or want for others. In effect, this becomes asking God for certain 'products' or, at least, set outcomes: 'Please God, let me have a PlayStation for Christmas' and, 'Please make my Nana's leg better.' While everyone is prone to this type of prayer to some extent, if this mindset defines children's understanding of prayer, then they may be particularly disappointed when God fails to provide the PlayStation or literal healing. A misunderstanding about this kind of prayer could tempt children to dismiss prayer, and God.

An emphasis on the nature of prayer as *process* is helpful here, for example, modelling petitionary prayer where the emphasis is on asking for God to help Nana as she struggles with her poorly leg. Then as children become able to talk about their understanding of prayer, it can be useful to help them distinguish between *prayer as a means to producing certain 'ends'* (to stop wars, to heal the sick, etc.) and *prayer as a valuable process* of reflection and discernment in God's presence.

Imagination and prayer

Giving permission to children to use their imagination and spontaneity can help to establish that prayer can sometimes be like an informal conversation with God – a conversation in which words might not be used by either party, but in which images and gestures play important roles. Moreover, children can be helped to see that, just as in the imaginative process, there may be important periods of waiting, silence and stillness where you don't know what might happen next.

These messages probably need to be repeatedly (and imaginatively!) emphasized because for many children public worship (in church or at school) is the main source of prayer experiences. That can lead to children forming the impression that prayer is necessarily a rather formal matter and needs to follow a set procedure in order for God to listen. The legacy of this misapprehension is often found in adults who as children missed out on learning that it is okay for prayer (especially personal, private prayer) to be much freer.

Imagination, however, is not necessarily the antithesis of structure. In supporting children's prayer life there is a need for both imagination and structure. It's intriguing that when the disciples asked Jesus to teach them to pray, he gave them a fairly clear formula (the Lord's Prayer), whereas more often than not when he was asked questions, he responded with just more questions! So why the prayer 'formula'?[12]

At any age, spiritual life can benefit from some structure and good reference points. Adopting a form need not condemn spontaneity, but the form can act as a tool that facilitates fresh expressions of prayer each time. So much about spiritual life involves surprises, ambiguity, mystery and creativity, that having a certain number of known reference points can give us confidence to go farther and deeper. Likewise, a certain amount of structure and routine can make a real contribution to a child's happiness and capacity to learn more in general.

So on some occasions the Lord's Prayer might be the appropriate formula to share with children when they are 'ready and ask'. We might bear in mind, though, that this prayer was offered as a help for adults. If it turns out that we need to do quite a bit of further teaching and interpretation of that prayer for children, then it is obviously not functioning as a simple enough basis or formula to get them going, and is not something they can really use here and now. It may be that prayers of this kind unhelpfully emphasize the 'set protocol' attitude to prayer.

The 'first prayers' children learn, therefore, need to have the overall character of a formula that they can easily take in and use as a spiritual tool. The formula is also a springboard for more, not an end in itself.

The 'formula' might be about using particular words or images, gestures, spaces, or the silences between these, a sense of beginning and ending, and some structuring of time to both listen and speak, give and take. This basic shape or structure might then grow as the child grows to include more words or more silence and have room for distinctive intentions of praise, confession or intercession. The point is that children begin with a currently helpful, spiritually genuine, formula of prayer, the properties of which they should never need to 'unlearn' at some later date. It needs to be something they can use and rely on now, and something that they can refer back to and build from at any future stage.

Think and discuss . . .

- What prayer shape or formula are children offered in your settings?
- Is the start of prayer time marked in any way (e.g. the lighting of a candle, sitting down)?
- How does it end?
- What is allowed to happen in the middle? What is not allowed to happen in the middle?
- How is imagination encouraged?

Relationship and prayer

Prayer is in itself a form of relating – of intentionally seeking a closer relationship with God – so the patterns we set for relating when we are with children are bound to affect their approach to prayer. In our relationships with the children in our churches, especially when prayer takes place, we need to strive for the same qualities that we hope the child's experience of 'being with God' will have.

This means that in our human relationships in the Sunday school, in the all-age service or domestic settings we should try to avoid treating others in ways that coerce or pressurize, mock, judge or reward. By striving for relationships based on unconditional love, rather than on a culture of praise, admiration or punishment, you can make a valuable contribution to the child's understanding of spiritual relationship. Psychoanalyst Alice Miller suggests that praise and admiration are, in any case, addictive toxins. Once you start, more and more is needed to achieve satisfaction. If the style of relating that children experience at church is of the 'just as I am' variety, they will much more readily enjoy that quality of God's relationship with them.[13]

Think and discuss . . .

- In what ways could children perceive a reward culture operating in your setting?
- As wider society tends to operate by reward culture standards, how can your church help the children to learn counter-cultural values of relating to one another unconditionally? Is doing that a kind of prayer?

Intimacy and prayer

Children's prayers are sometimes treated very differently from the prayers offered by adults. It's not uncommon to hear children's prayers quoted as a kind of entertaining sermon illustration, or even to find whole books making fun of how 'cute' and 'wonky' children's prayers can be. The practice of children 'coming up to share their prayers' in all-age worship also needs to be very sensitively managed to ensure that this does not become a form of sweet entertainment for the grown ups or at least feel like that to the children. If children's prayer is used in this way, it seriously disrupts the intimate nature of prayer, and of spiritual life in general. Children need protection from the hijacking of their prayers for use in public moments that are disconnected from the context in which their prayer was made. We do not do this to adults, and it is unacceptable to do it to those less able to object for themselves.

Another important way in which we can support intimacy in children's developing prayer life is by doing as much as possible to emphasize that prayer is *not* just about putting thoughts into words, especially the written word. Again, this can be a challenge when children's prayers are included in all-age worship where typically the spotlight is given to verbalized prayer. Inadvertently, this has the potential to teach children that less value is given to more intimate kinds of prayer such as prayer that is so heartfelt that it doesn't use words or is about something so difficult that it can't be put into words.

Trust and prayer

Trust plays a key role in providing conditions that nurture children's prayer life. It is about trusting that a child may be praying even if we can't be sure that this is happening. Just as adults, sometimes, can give the outward signs of praying even though little may really be going on inside, children can give the outward signs of *not* praying, according to our criteria, but perhaps a lot is going on inside.

So we need to take a generous, trusting attitude to what may constitute prayerful activity for children. It may look as if a child is just doodling or idly rolling balls of play dough or gazing blankly out of the window (rather than producing a facsimile drawing of the Bible story or listening attentively to us) but in these moments God and the child may be in deep communion. And so it is important to treat what they are up to with the respect with which we'd treat someone deep in prayer, and avoid disturbing or interrogating them.

> I pray in my head, talking to myself and God whenever I'm lonely, every day really.
>
> (boy aged five)

> On my new trampoline I jump to the clouds and then God listens and I hear him too.
>
> (boy aged four)

This trusting attitude will not only nurture that possibility into reality some of the time, but also send important messages to all the children about who and how we trust. For example, in the Godly Play approach leaders explain that children should avoid barging into or shouting across one another out of respect for the other person's engagement with God, rather than simply for social reasons. To be told often: 'Be careful that you don't disturb someone who may be speaking with God here' builds up a powerful expectation of the reality and mystery of what prayer is.

Think and discuss . . .

- What is your best experience of prayer with children?
- What is your worst?

- How will your understanding of children's spirituality help you approach prayer now:

    (a)   with children

    (b)   in your own prayer life?

Using the Bible
Accessibility

The Bible is not an easily accessible resource for children. Countless versions, adaptations and 'takes' are now offered to get around this problem and to make it more child-friendly. Some of these succeed better than others, but often the aim of appealing to children is made on the assumption that neither children nor the Bible have profound spiritual qualities. For example, stories are selected on the basis of their suspected natural appeal to children, such as all the ones with animals (Noah, Daniel and the lions' den, Jonah and the whale, the prodigal son) or those with smaller people as heroes (David and Goliath, Zacchaeus, the boy with the loaves and fishes). And stories are often retold by fluffy animals, cartoon characters or comical puppets. The depth of the stories is quickly reduced to a 'simple message', usually a moral or take-home 'teaching'. And the complexity of both the child and the story is treated as a nuisance or at least something to be got round, rather than a vital ingredient. This may be missing the point about both.

Interaction and response

One way of engaging children is to make Bible stories *more interactive*. This seems a sound principle. Many adults are painfully passive in their reactions to deeply incongruent or disturbing Bible passages. Often adults cease to notice what puzzles them and what they would have liked to ask or explore about familiar stories, especially in relation to their own life story. So forming an interactive habit, a response habit, as early as possible is a good idea. Children's propensity to ask awkward questions and the freshness of their approach to material that's overly familiar to the church are qualities to be nurtured, not discouraged.

But sometimes in Bible storytelling 'interaction' can be done for its own sake, without thought for the spiritual implications. For example, to present the story of Jonah to children, a storyteller invited them to 'groan and moan' as loudly as they could every time Jonah heard God speaking. This succeeded in keeping the children's attention, but created two (contradictory) strong associations with that story. First, this device was used so many times that there was a danger that the predominant message the children would be left with from this story would be a negative view of God (response to God = groan). And, secondly, it was easy for the volume of the groaning to get louder and sillier, leaving the children with the impression that the crux of this story is hilarity. Clearly the *verbal* message the storyteller was hoping to convey was quite different, but actions (and feelings) speak louder than words, especially to children.[14]

Godly Play

Many find that the Godly Play approach to using the Bible with children takes the spiritual character of both children and the Bible material more seriously. Godly Play takes into account children's need for accessible language. It also addresses their need to develop habits of interaction and response to the biblical material. In Godly Play:

- The stories are told in a fairly straight way (without resorting to additional characters or gimmicks) in the belief that the emotional depth of these great narratives will speak directly to children's own experience of emotional depth. Godly Play takes the view that children's existential needs and the biblical material are well met as both are concerned with major issues – identity, freedom, power, good and evil, love and care.[15]

- Rather than 'jazzing things up', the delivery is considerably slowed down to allow the child time to get inside this complexity rather than skate across its surface. The words and images in each story are treated with reverence, what is serious is taken seriously, what is joyful is treated joyfully, etc.

- The story is told without a book, from the heart, with relatively few, but carefully chosen, words and phrases. Gestures are used sparingly to mark especially important moments or themes – such as holding a hand as if in blessing over a key character to whom God is very close. There is time and space to dwell in the story.

- The story, rather than the storyteller, is made the spiritual focus of the telling. The children's eye gaze is directed away from the storyteller's face towards carefully selected three-dimensional, child-hand-sized images that portray key motifs in the story.

- Using these images (rather than a book) means that at the end the children are left with a physical representation of the whole story – not just the last scene, which is often not the spiritual key to the story. The images also encourage children, even non-readers, to retell and play out the story for themselves, getting inside its meaning in their own ways, perhaps in line with their own spiritual signature and current needs.

Many of these techniques can be adopted in any Bible story situation with children, but many extensively researched, theologically considered, Godly Play scripts are available and are well worth making use of (see www.godlyplay.org.uk).

Developing a sense of wonder

In Godly Play, interactive response to the story is especially encouraged and nurtured so that over time this becomes the children's habitual response to all biblical material. Following every telling of the story, a clearly signalled period is set aside for 'wondering' about what has just been heard. This is deliberately open-ended, and is sensitively facilitated to give the children permission to identify their feelings, questions and insights in response to the story experience. It is not like the typical group discussion in which the leader selects favoured responses in order to reach a predetermined teaching point. All responses are treated as valid, even negative ones. Developing the children's habit of responding authentically, rather than second guessing how the teacher wants them to respond, is seen as the spiritual goal.

In this wondering process, children also learn that there are many important differences in the ways people react and respond to each Bible story, and the children learn to respect the variety of ways people make meaning. The interactive process allows for the individuality of spiritual life to be honoured; there is no herding into a common consensus. If a story, for example, of the Passover before the exodus from Egypt, has made one child angry, but another delighted, this difference is recognized as very important and to be respected. This helps to open up the children's sense of the infinite possibilities of meaning that biblical material holds for their spiritual life in the long term. In other words, everything possible is done to avoid studying the Bible with children in ways that suggest *this* story has *this* point and once you've learned this, there's nothing more in it. Children's own honest reactions are invited and developed, and they also benefit from hearing the honest reactions of others – a rich mix of interactive response.

Finally, the interactive approach of Godly Play to Bible stories moves beyond a discussion-based response to other means of interacting further with the experience. Children are offered a period of time in which they have free choice in how to pursue how the story has affected them – through drawing, making, painting, reading, writing and, of course, playing. The children are not given set activities (draw this or make that), but learn to use these media to contemplate and discover their reactions in different, less verbal and perhaps more private, forms than was possible in the group discussion.

Spiritual diet

Another notable feature of the Godly Play approach is its attention to a 'balanced spiritual diet' for children, for example, by providing a reasonable selection from both Old and New Testament stories. Godly Play also distinguishes between historical and other kinds of narrative (such as parables) and offers story-like presentations of key Christian traditions – including baptism, the Church seasons, Holy Communion, Lent and Advent. By contrast, such as where churches follow a three-year lectionary approach, children's biblical diet is sometimes determined by what the *adults* need. And once realistic choices have been made about which of the three readings to focus on in the children's work (perhaps not the Leviticus one?), the resulting menu can be limited to just the New Testament for a long stretch in a child's life.

Also with an eye to what might be required for a *child's* spiritual nourishment, Godly Play makes a point of regularly revisiting menu favourites or 'staples'. This repetition is a valuable way of helping children enter more deeply into the layers of meaning that are in each story, and find, within the same story, told in the same familiar way, a variety of their own experiences. Novelty for its own sake can become a disruption to the process of coming back again, but seeing new things, that communicates something about our trust in the Bible to accompany our spiritual life whatever our age.

Space, **P**rocess, **I**magination, **R**elationship, **I**ntimacy, **T**rust

The six criteria for auditing spirituality-nurturing practice apply to the use of the Bible just as much as to any other area of practice. In the Godly Play approach, for example, sensitivity to the spiritual quality of Bible storytelling does not lie just in the telling. It depends also on thoughtfully creating an inviting, *intimate space* in which that storytelling might happen. For example, it can be helpful to take all the sets of images from previous stories shared with the children and set them out on accessible shelves around the room or space. This helps children appreciate that these are not stories in isolation, but part of a much greater whole. It allows them to choose to revisit any story, and make connections between the story told that day and those told previously.

Following the telling of a story, the children are encouraged to play freely, *imaginatively*, with any of the images. This conveys an unusual absence of adult control, and is the intention to *trust*. In other words, the stories are told not as discrete ends in themselves or standalone 'teaching points' but rather as stories that point children to an infinite *process* of connection and meaning, to God. The emphasis on 'pointing' rather than 'showing' is vital. The style of *relationship* between the storyteller and the children matters too, so establishing a good sense of community, feeling 'ready' both personally and collectively, is seen as essential preparation to any storytelling.

Think and discuss . . .

- Which Bible stories do you recall most clearly from your childhood?
- How were they told?
- What struck you most about them?
- Do you think they appealed to any spiritual needs you had at that time?
- If so, was anyone else aware of that?

This chapter, together with Chapter 4, has tackled ways in which children's ministry can respond, in practical terms, to the needs of children's spirituality. In this chapter, the focus has been specifically on prayer and Bible storytelling, but you will also have picked up on implications for our approach to worship and Christian nurture in the home. The next chapter considers some of the underlying theology about childhood. The intention is not to turn away from practice, but to offer a way to build even stronger foundations, and where necessary provide good arguments for challenging unspiritual practices.

6 Christian imagery and thought about children

This chapter outlines a few intersections between Christian theology and children's spirituality. It could be inspiration for further reading, as the theological contributions are only briefly covered here.

Knowledge of some theological elements might also be useful when presenting your case (to your team, your parish council, etc) that children's spirituality needs our attention. This can equip you not only to cover the points made in our earlier chapters – that empirical evidence shows that spirituality is an everyday part of children's lives; that there are educational and psychological reasons for wanting to address this issue; and that models of good spiritual practice are on hand to try out – but also to draw on the significant streams in Christian thought that draw attention to the primacy of spirituality in childhood.

Childhood and 'theological attention deficit'

In the last hundred years or more, a huge amount of material has been written about childhood. Literally hundreds of different theories have analysed the factors that influence and define childhood. However, in comparison to other disciplines (such as psychology, sociology or education), theology has contributed very little to this debate. Possibly the subject of childhood has been seen by Christian theologians as beneath them, primarily an area for practitioners. Yet even in preparing men and women for the practical tasks of Christian ministry, theological colleges pay very little attention to childhood.

As a consequence, churches can be awash with a confusing mixture of images and ideas about what 'being a child' really means from a Christian perspective. Many of these images and ideas are unspoken, even unconscious. Others may be built on a narrow or too simplistic foundation – perhaps a single Bible verse. Any theological grasp on childhood in such Christian contexts and communities is often a matter of chance. The ideal of theology being a means of sifting through the complexity of ideas about, and human experience of, God and then suggesting some logical ways of holding all the meaning together, is a distant ideal when childhood is not even recognized as a mainstream subject for theological reflection. Despite all this, the small amount of theology that is directed towards childhood gives some very significant arguments for putting children's spirituality centre stage.

Think and discuss . . .

- How is 'childhood' considered a part of the theological work of your congregation?
- How could it be more than a 'minority' interest that focuses on the practical tasks of children's work and only for those who perform those tasks?
- Could childhood feature as a topic in Lent courses, Alpha-type courses, the work of home groups, or in a parish retreat?
- Have a look at themes explored in your church's previous lay education programmes. What effect might deliberately including questions about childhood have had (in the discussion of, for example, salvation, the cross, evangelism, prayer or using the Bible)? (Not simply, 'How would you talk to children about this?' but, 'What does your understanding of salvation have to say about childhood, and vice versa?)

Imagery

The range of Christian imagery about childhood is diverse and often pulls in two or more directions. This in itself reminds us that paradox is at the heart of childhood. A child is both 'now' and a suggestion of what is developing. The paradoxes in Christian imagery make it clear that it would be futile, even wrong, to simplify what childhood means by turning it into something one dimensional.

Marcia Bunge explores the many biblical images associated with childhood as follows:

Children in the Bible are:

gifts from God	*but also*	burdens, responsibilities (like widows and orphans)
models of innocence ('for such is the kingdom')	*but also*	unreconstructed pre Christian and primitive savages in original sin
knowing/prophetic ('out of the mouths of babes')[17]	*but also*	in need of teaching ('teach your children')

The complex, contrary elements in the biblical imagery underline how hard it is to establish an understanding on which to build good children's work practices and education. Most churches have both explicit and implicit images depicting children. Sometimes the images conflict without our realizing it, and this confusion may scupper attempts to get to grips with children's spirituality. Why not explore this in your context? For instance, where are images of children seen in your church and what kind of images are they? Maybe there are children in the stained glass or other church artwork. What impression of childhood do these capture – vulnerable, loving, dependent, idealized? Are only adults represented in the imagery?

There are also images in the words, and sometimes actions, of our worship. Is the congregation referred to as 'children of God' only in the context of confession of sin and dependence? At what point are real children 'visual images'? What images come across? Perhaps it's the image of children escaping to their groups like animals released from a cage. Or as gift bearers during the offertory. Or as entertainers or a light relief in the 'show and tell' after the serious part of the service. Or relegated to the back pews or area out of sight where it doesn't matter what they do. Are they allowed to sit together in one place, perhaps at the front, or does this feel more of a requirement? Whose benefit is that really for? (In one church a 'cry area' for restless babies and toddlers was referred to as 'the sin bin', by the churchwarden. The ramifications of this imagery are striking!)

Becoming more aware of the messages about children provided in church and Christian imagery is an important step towards supporting children's spirituality. Sometimes what we are trying to say in words and policies is at odds with our imagery, and that makes change difficult. For example, taking the spiritual voice of the child more seriously could be harder where most of the imagery of childhood is of the helpless, sleeping baby Jesus. Or it may be difficult to sustain a sense that children's spirituality also has things to offer the wider community when most of the imagery portrays children as 'takers' or 'in need'.

But imagery can also be a good way of holding on to contrasting, even conflicting, ideas. Real children need more than an idealized, perfect set of imagery in which to find themselves, and where we can find them. Their reality is messy: made up of having a voice *and* wanting to listen; spiritual intuition *and* incomprehension of half our words; being people in their own right *and* dependent on others. They do 'sleep sweetly', but they also do make plenty of noise crying (unlike the 'little Lord Jesus, no crying he makes' image in the carol).

To do justice to children's spiritual lives, we need to be more aware of our imagery and to see it as a powerful way in which to engage with issues of paradox and complexity. Images can be a good way of counteracting simplistic thinking.

Images and ideas in theology
The child as holy sacrament
Some argue that one meaning of childhood lies in its capacity to be sacramental: that a child is a sacrament of God. At one level, the incarnation seems to support this idea. God takes not just human form, but the form of a child. This opens distinct meanings to be explored further.

At another level, Jesus invited his followers to treat children sacramentally. He offers us ordinary bread and wine and says that when we receive these we receive him. He also took an ordinary child, saying, 'Whoever welcomes this child in my name welcomes me, and whoever welcomes me welcomes the one who sent me' (Luke 9.48). In Chris Jamber's view this is virtually the institution of another sacrament: 'Jesus is the sacrament of God, the child is the sacrament of Jesus. Children are "thin places" where the mystical clue to the presence of the divine can break through.'[18]

Think and discuss . . .

For many Christians, the sacraments, such as receiving the bread and wine in the sacrament of Holy Communion, are key spiritual encounters.

- What would it take for the 'reception of', or relationships with, children to have similar spiritual qualities and expectations?
- Has this ever happened to you?
- What objections or obstacles might there be to this kind of thinking?

Suffering and fragility

David Jensen, a theologian in the Reformed Church, suggests that the suffering or hurting child has a special significance for Christian understanding. God gives his own child to the world, a child who will be hurt and broken – an ultimate symbol of vulnerability and of grace. Jensen comments that we may be able to come a little closer to that truth about God by coming closer to the reality of children's experiences of hurt and brokenness today.

Of course, coming closer to the negative, hurtful experiences children face provokes an ethical reaction and response – we might identify things we can *do* to help. But there is also a spiritual challenge in this theological analysis: that is, to recognize the ways we unintentionally support a world, or just a Church, that is prone to hurt and break its most vulnerable.

The symbolism of our redemption being contingent on the role of a child, that is, God's son, not the father alone, is also an invitation for reflection. Where the 'child' in all kinds of senses is left out or deemed unnecessary, is there a danger of short-changing a fuller theological understanding – of creation, of salvation, of justice, and the rest? Maybe times exist when we consider it better to exclude children – perhaps to protect them from experiences we judge to be inappropriate for them (e.g. communion, baptism, a funeral). No doubt the protective father in God wanted to avoid Jesus needing to take up his role in redemption, but perhaps the lesson is that the child is essential.

Think and discuss . . .

Think about a child you know who has had to endure particularly hurtful experiences (poverty, ill health, a broken home).

- How is this child's vulnerability a window on God's grace?
- How does your church understand its vocation to such children and their protection? Is it focused on acknowledging the child's experience, or on distracting the child from it? How do you think your church feels towards that child (or would feel if she or he came)?

Joy and wonder

Roman Catholic theologian Sofia Cavalletti has a strong sense of the child's profound spiritual instincts and needs. She developed her strong Christian understanding of the child through close observations of children. This is an under-used strategy we could all better employ: simply observing children in order to ask ourselves how does what we see (or don't see) tells us something about their capacity for spirituality, and also to ask what we learn about God from such observation. This includes observation of their ordinary activities – at play, in conversation, as they drop off to sleep or puzzle something out – as well as explicitly religious activity.

Cavalletti's observations have identified *deep joy* and a sense of *pure wonder* as core strengths in children's spirituality capacities. An ordinary example might be a toddler becoming totally absorbed in watching snow falling. Cavalletti believes that these states of joy and wonder also characterize children's capacity to 'fall in love with God' in the most natural, uncoerced way. What matters is that this kind of joy and wonder should be supported in experiences of Christian life by providing conditions that offer children security, comfort and peace.

Deep joy is distinguished from general happiness by its tendency towards stillness rather than excited activity. Pure wonder precedes the more adult-like ability to 'wonder about' this or that. The child's wonder is closer to an attitude of contemplation, often silent, especially when the child does not yet have much verbal language.

For Cavalletti, as for many others, a vital aspect of spiritual nurture is looking after what the child already has rather than rushing to put 'in' what they appear not to have. Being pushed prematurely to consider something in a rather intellectual way or, worse still, being told what think, will disconnect children from their capacity for deep joy and pure wonder in religious life. Rather than 'falling in love with God', value is misplaced on to learning about God and about love. The result can be proficient religious knowledge but a faint spiritual pulse.[19]

Think and discuss . . .

Set aside five to ten minutes to observe a child or infant in any ordinary context (e.g. the park, on a bus, playing at home).

● What glimpses do you get of characteristics that could also be spiritual qualities?

● If this child is 'made in the image of God', what do you learn about God?

Blessing

Jerome Berryman is one of the most influential of the contemporary Christian thinkers on childhood, religious nature and nurture. He is also the originator of the Godly Play approach.[20] He proposes the theological theme of *blessing* as a key concept around which to organize thought and practice in children's ministry.

Following Jesus' example, children's spiritual status calls for blessing rather than judgement or adjustment. Whereas adults are enjoined to follow, change, be born again or become like children, *actual* children are not addressed in this way. They are simply welcomed and blessed, as in the story related in Matthew 19.13-15. This supports a 'high view' of children's spiritual life as already valid, regardless of age or stage of knowledge.

With blessing as a key to a theological understanding of childhood, interesting challenges arise for the tasks of ministry with children – teaching, evangelism, care and nurture, worship. It is easy for our approaches to these to slip from being 'about blessing' to being about trying to *change, control or manipulate* the children – judging them by what they lack, rather than blessing what they are.

Berryman is clear, however, that this blessing must be realistic, not idealistic. He suggests that it is just as dangerous to put children and childhood on a pedestal as it to underestimate or miss chances to recognize their spiritual capacities. Blessing, 'benediction', literally means 'to call out the good'. So our approach needs to be sensitive to calling out the good that is really there, rather than that we'd like to project on to children. To call out what is 'really there', however, requires more than theory or theology about childhood; it needs a close relationship with children as unique individuals. This demands practical theology at its most practical. It is perhaps no wonder that in the past many theologians have crossed the road rather than come face to face with these issues!

Play

Play – a more unusual theological theme – is key in Berryman's view of childhood spirituality. He suggests that the playful game of hide and seek, or peekaboo (a game even the smallest child enters into), is an apt metaphor for our experience of God throughout our lives. Play is described as a natural language of childhood, and therefore a vital creative process through which Christian language can take root in the child's life.

But the fact that good play is satisfying, done largely for its own sake (a process rather than a product), can draw us into uncharted waters (imagination, deeper relationships), and can't be forced, is suggestive of things at the heart of Christian spiritual life too. So play has certain sacred qualities, which in turn are at the heart of a child's life. This recommends that we should particularly look out for the sacred in play, and be more alert to playfulness in the sacred.

Think and discuss . . .

- For some, 'play' is not naturally associated with God, theology or the Church. Why do you think that is?
- Are there occasions when the Church plays? If so, what is significant about those moments?
- How was Jesus playful in his approach to ministry?
- Does God play? How, and with whom?

Relationship

A main point for Berryman about childhood spirituality is the way it calls for us to enter into genuine and open relationships with children. Jesus' instruction was that people should become like children, but he did not define what childhood is meant to illustrate, nor what it is about children in general that our spiritual lives should emulate. So for Berryman, the task Jesus sets can only be tackled by exploring our own particular relationships with children and our relationship with our own childlikeness. It is not a task that can be adequately covered by reading textbooks about childhood or by trying to ascertain what childhood was in the time of Jesus, or what defines it in modern children. The deep meaning of 'becoming like a child' comes best from each relationship we have with each child and the face of God that we see in the child's face in that moment. Relationship is not something you study and at some point 'get'. Rather, it is a never-ending journey of discovery. So the task is not to have an intellectual debate on the question, 'What does being childlike really mean?', but to seek insight through relating with children (and the child within us).

This emphasis is also important because it reminds us of the pointlessness of trying to understand children in isolation (though to a large extent child psychology and other disciplines have until recently focused too much on the discrete subject of children). Nor can we get far by putting them, or 'their' spirituality, under the microscope – another form of isolation that flies in the face of the reality of their lives, which is so much about relationships and their constantly changing dynamic. This refers us back to Chapter 1, and the research-based way of defining children's spirituality as 'relational consciousness', that is, especially found in the child's emerging awareness of themselves in relation to others, the world, and God.[21]

Dark and light

Some views of childhood emphasize all that is good and innocent. Other views point to a darker side, suggesting that childhood is a period of primitive impulses and irrational emotions. In popular imagery, even now, portrayals of children lurch between images of little cherubs and little devils.[22]

Over the centuries, Christian thought about children has also been swayed both ways, resulting in some practices that seem unimaginable for Christians today. For example, John Wesley suggested that part of Christian nurture involved 'breaking the small child's will' by force, including physical force. And in the nineteenth century, some Christian educators advocated a 'frighten them into belief' approach, with dreadful accounts and images of hell that emphasized all that is wrong with the human condition, temptation, sin and the reality of the devil.

It can be tempting to react by pointing young children wholly towards the good and the light in Christian theology. Indeed, Sofia Cavalletti suggests that young children (under the age of six) should not be exposed to Old Testament stories in which God is at times angry and destructive, nor even the more frightening aspects of the parable of the good shepherd (the threat of the wolf and the hired hand).

However, the majority of contemporary thinkers who study children's spirituality and its relationship to Christian theology do not agree with Cavalletti about this. Gretchen Wolff-Pritchard makes a strong case for children of all ages needing some of the darker language and imagery to furnish their spiritual life with the depth that they already know from experience. She laments the ways children are sometimes given edited, sanitized, 'smiley' bits of the Bible, rather than being provided with appropriate ways of engaging with its stories in their full, emotionally complex form. Even Easter can be an example of this editing, with children being 'spared' the story of Good Friday while expected to engage with the meaning of Easter.[23]

Berryman shares this view that children of all ages have no less need of the darker material. Children are hungry for a language to address their complex experiences and sense of life. To do justice to this, their spirituality needs more than a language of love. The Christian language tradition has a huge richness to offer, and, arguably, if we hide the darker religious language from them, children will seek it in other places. They might infer that the reality of all that they are and know of (the good and the bad) is not really addressed in Christian dialogue.

Abiding reality

German theologian Karl Rahner describes childhood as an 'abiding reality', working on the point that we are called not so much to grow out of our childhood as to grow *into* it.[24]

What would it mean to engage with childhood as an 'abiding reality'? A lot of messages tell us that childhood is largely without value, something to be got through as quickly as possible. Pressure is put on children to grow up too fast (to be cleverer than average for their age, to look or dress like adults, to have adult-type relationships), which inevitably diminishes the value of childhood. Rowan Williams points out that many children need to have time set aside *not* to be adult, a sanctuary from adult responsibilities. Christians need to recapture this understanding of childhood, and be advocates for valuing childhood as more than merely a means to an end. Ultimately, this may help adults to value the childlike in themselves, not simply in some shallow, nostalgic sense, but with a deep respect for childhood's defining paradox of being *and* becoming.

This brief account of how theology has been engaging with childhood shows that that discussion is made up of many different themes. Not surprisingly, childhood resists simplistic theological treatment. The more you think about the theological issues, the more questions and debates open up. This should be taken as a sign of an area ripe for more attention, from which practical ministry will stand to benefit. The temptation to put all the effort into the practical design and delivery of children's ministry needs to be resisted, even if that practice puts more emphasis on children's spirituality. Theological effort is needed, both to inform and to critique what we do. It can help us to see 'why' and 'why not'.

In this chapter we have seen that there is good theological support for taking the spiritual character of childhood very seriously. If our mindset continues to shift *towards* children's spirituality, and *away from* treating children's religious nurture merely as a matter of teaching them what they don't know or disguising immense truths in snack-sized nuggets, then hopefully even more theological voices will be attracted by the opportunity to join in. Even if it's messy.

Think and discuss . . .

- It has been suggested that much of our theology is learned from hymns. How is childhood treated in the hymns, choruses and songs in your church?
- Look at songs used especially with children, and at hymns sung by the congregation as a whole. Can you spot any themes from this chapter in these hymns and songs?

7 Frequently asked questions

If spirituality thrives on a less 'teachy' approach, what is my role and how will I know if I've made any impression?
This book has suggested that children's spirituality can be sidelined, even closed down, by the side effects of our teaching. There has been a repeated critique of the spiritual fall-out from approaches that measure success in terms of getting teaching points across, however entertainingly that is done.

We are not the first to struggle with the complexity of Christian nurture or to have been distracted by other important foci. The primary emphasis has rarely been spiritual. For example, early Sunday schools were focused on making a *social* difference, addressing poverty and inequality. Today, the social impetus might be to provide clubs where children can play safely while their parents work, or to provide support networks for young mums with toddlers. But the key focus has often been to make an *educational* difference: in the past the Church provided basic instruction to children who might not otherwise have learned to read and write. And now the Church sometimes sees its task as providing religious knowledge to children who may not otherwise get this at home or in school.

But providing religious knowledge is not a prerequisite for *spiritual* life. In fact, there are ways of acquiring and using religious knowledge that might be detrimental to spiritual health. It could become a largely intellectual exercise and be about acquiring expertise, about knowing more than others, rather than a way of being able to love others, and love God.

The problem is that it is relatively easy to demonstrate whether or not we've made an impact on children's religious knowledge. To focus on spirituality, by contrast, can make us feel uncertain about ourselves (and worried about what others might think of us), and unsure about whether or not the children have benefited. It might help if you redefine your role in terms of spiritual mentor, guide or director rather than 'teacher' or 'leader'. This may clarify the fact that knowledge, knowledge transfer, expertise and authority are much less important as criteria and objectives for *spiritual* teaching and learning.

When evaluating your work with children you will therefore need to ask a different kind of question: 'Ask not what the children have learned from you, but what you have learned from them/being with them'![25] This will help you to focus on the spiritual, rather than on the transfer of information. By looking at teaching and learning in this upside down sort of way, you are likely to see that the children *are* learning lots. This should desensitize you to the pressure of conventional learning assessments of the story or theme you have set up for the day. And it should help you to notice ways in which other kinds of (unexpected) learning occurred as you all responded to the opportunity of the present moment, for example, spiritual learning about 'being church', living with respect for differences, encountering God, being authentic and being excited by the fertility of Christian language to make new meanings.

How is spirituality affected by changes in the ways children think?

To improve the child-friendliness of their work with children, churches emulate the age-divided, age-appropriate approach to intellectual development that is followed by schools.

Child psychology has demonstrated that children's minds are not just like adults' minds but with 'less inside'! Children's *ways* of thinking are different. In infancy they draw first on bodily experience ('sensori-motor thought'), then from about the age of two on feelings and images. By about the age of six, thinking is often most easily collected in story and literal patterns. Finally, from about eleven years, abstract, conceptual ways of putting ideas together become more natural and efficient. Many church programmes follow these patterns to ensure that what is offered to children has the best chance of appealing to their natural ways of learning and thinking.[26]

Learning information and being able to turn ideas around is often well served by this developmentally sensitive approach. But it is not inevitable that *spirituality* is subject to the same restrictions. There's a real danger here of making the error of over-identifying spirituality and intellectual ability. We need to take seriously the alternative – that spirituality might have less to do with age, intellect and mental life, and much more with being and feeling.

This book has suggested that spirituality has something to do with being sensitive to the presence of God, and with having an awareness of wider connections that invite us into acts of creative meaning-making and help us to fend off a sense of meaninglessness. Does this depend on reaching a particular developmental milestone? Could this not occur just as much through sensori-motor 'thought'?

So while not completely rejecting the developmental nuances, it's important to be wary of the traps they can lay for us. For example, it's dangerous to assume that later ways of thinking and knowing are 'better', and that the ways a child thinks and knows about spiritual matters right now are of less value, just something to put up with.

Does spirituality develop?

The term 'spiritual development' is problematic. It is quite hard to think of development without imagining a linear, hierarchical model. But that kind of model does not fit spirituality, which does *not* necessarily go from less to more, from simple to complex. And linear thinking can make it hard to value 'earlier' stages in spiritual development as highly as later stages.

But spirituality can certainly be impeded, crushed, thwarted – stopped from developing. It can go underground too. Some children in our research described interiorizing it, secluding it to a private domain that they did not plan to share or working to replace it with other 'more useful' things.[27] So nurture matters: spirituality is not a constant, nor something that will develop and grow regardless of what we do.

Getting to grips with children's spirituality means deliberately letting go of our normal criteria for development. It is not about how much children have learned, what they have made or how close to the 'ideal' they have moved (e.g. assessing to what extent they now 'understand' the Eucharist). Spiritual development requires both a much longer-term view and also a much more immediate-term view of growth.

The immediate-term view is about asking, 'How is this experience, right now, a positive, that is, developing, experience of God for this child or these children?' Note that this might not have much to do with the content of the session or conversation. It might be more about the feel of the session, the relationships, or perhaps how conflict was handled or the way space was created and respected for each person to speak and be heard. These will be key moments of spiritual learning and possible leaps in understanding about Christian ways of being with one another and with God.

The longer-term view invites us to notice habits that might be developing much more slowly, shaping the child's lifelong spiritual attitude. This could be children's inclination to wonder, to think reflectively or to value thinking for themselves – all active rather than passive spiritual habits. They could build up gradually, through encouragement of honest, affective responses to biblical study. But it might take a long time, as most children are more used to a 'right answer' culture from their experience of school. Or spiritual development might be evident, over time, in an increasing ability to listen to others and be enriched by their very different responses, that is, discovering they are part of a journeying, developing community rather than pursuing merely a personal faith path. To 'see' this kind of spiritual development, you need to consider changes over months or even longer.

How does age affect spirituality?
Spirituality calls for a mindset that sees the child's capacities rather than their handicaps. At each age, the child has natural inclinations that lend themselves to spiritual strengths. This can mean that bringing together quite a mixed age group of children allows for much richer experiences for all, the strengths of each age complementing the others.

The youngest children (0–3)
- Can be open to *embodied kinds of knowing* (which might be a sense of God through touch, movement, warmth or light);
- can have an acute sensitivity to the *here and now*;
- may have moments of an overwhelming kind of blurred knowing that Freud described as 'oceanic feeling' where their weak sense of 'I' (ego) is dramatically contrasted to a sense of the hugeness of everything else, an *intuition of the infinite* (a kind of mystical feeling);
- can be more attuned towards an *attitude of trust and hope*. Reliable, reassuring experiences of people and the way they mediate the infant's experiences of a (sometimes hostile) world build up this attitude. Soothing a crying baby with the 'it's all right' message, signals the

trust that the carer has in a much greater, transcendent quality to life, a message of *ultimate 'alrightness'*, and consequently an inclination to hopefulness.[28] Trust and hope are key themes in Christian thought, so a personal resonance with these facilitates spiritual engagement.

The small child (approximately 3–6)

- Has a pronounced sense of emotional life – wrestles with issues of power and powerlessness, guilt and initiation, self doubt and autonomy, and welcomes religious material that feeds this rather than trying to address needs for intellectual understanding; cares about *emotional meaning* rather than intellectual meaning;

- *sees things 'whole'* rather than analytically;

- is *at ease with knowing* without having to account for how one knows – growing in 'knowing God' is more appealing than knowing this or that 'about God'; *faith matters more than belief*;

- is free of pre-determined categories, so is more open to encountering God in all kinds of places and forms;

- has an *affinity with images/characters* to carry or make meaning, especially complex meaning (whereas stories do this for older children and religious concepts and doctrines may do that for adults), so is especially open to images/characters that address complex matters like good and evil, power and vulnerability, fear and safety.

The older child (approximately 7+)

- Becomes more aware of mental or *'inner life'* as different from external experiences;

- develops a *sense of conscience*, which can suggest an inner guide or reality beyond the everyday self and everyday inclinations;

- is concerned with *right and wrong*, judgement and justice;

- is *more interested in language* and words to name feelings and experiences; likes to categorize, but welcomes categories for things that transcend simple categories too (mystery, infinite, awesome, cosmic, ultimate)!

- can be *verbal (more public) about spiritual life* without being tied to the rules, refreshingly honest and imaginative in thinking things through;

- has developing capacity to *ask questions*, a desire to sort things out (though has less interest in getting answers that end this 'game');
- finds in *stories* an appealing way to explore complex emotional issues.[29]

Are boys different?

It is interesting how often this question is asked! It suggests that there is a popular expectation that there are significant gender issues that affect spirituality in childhood. The research evidence, however, has not provided much to support this idea. But assumptions can affect our practice and in turn affect the children, so it might be useful to explore what expectations you have about boy/girl differences. For example, do you think girls might be more spiritual than boys? Why?

Clearly, gender is a rather crude variable – just two options! This is an area in which we could become dangerously prejudiced and miss valuable diversity and individuality. In shaping our practice to assumptions about what girls like or what boys like, we might miss the reality of what they really are or could be. Some toy shops offer rather fixed views, but most people know that both boys and girls can get a lot from exploring life on the 'other side of the fence', girls playing with spider man, boys playing with dolls. Similarly, boys can really enjoy *some* opportunities to be reflective, less active and less competitive. If their usual culture provides few such opportunities, these can quite literally be 'sanctuary moments'.

One difference observed by some Godly Play practitioners is the type of engagement demonstrated by boys and girls. During the storytelling, girls more often appear to be thoughtful, still or absorbed while boys may always be interrupting and can seem more restless, distracted or dismissive. However, closer observation can yield some surprising results. This applies especially to the quality of responses shown by the children once they have been given the freedom to make their own choices about how to explore things for themselves. The boys, who appeared to be pretty disengaged, for whatever reason, are later highly focused as they pursue what sparked their interest, demonstrating that they missed nothing, and took things in at a deep level. The message about boys and their spirituality is perhaps that we should not judge by appearances.

It can be harder for girls to respond to the independence and freedom to choose for themselves. The culture of 'do something to please the teacher' seems to be alarmingly engrained in some girls, who would prefer a set activity. However, if spiritual life is about discovering for ourselves what we are being called to be and do, then there is value in facing the challenge of making our own response. Girls may need extra support to deal with the 'scary' open-endedness of free response time, and to learn that spiritual work is not done to please others and that *not knowing* what to do is an important experience in spiritual life, an experience to face rather than avoid.

How is spiritual nurture related to learning styles?

In schools today there is concern to cater for a variety of learning styles. Some children are visual learners; others may be auditory or kinaesthetic learners. If only one kind of learning style is catered for, then many children will be disadvantaged. In the context of Christian nurture, often the policy adopted to handle this is for everyone to do a bit of everything, So a range of activities is programmed to provide some time that is physical, some creative or arty and some verbal. The problem is that usually this divides the time children spend doing any one thing into much smaller units, so even when each child's particular learning style is attended to, it's far too brief to allow space for the deeper, absorbed work that spirituality thrives on. Instead, the children might be buffeted from one thing to the next, and feel that three-quarters of the time they are being required to develop spiritual responses in ways that are 'not very me'. The child-friendly intention to provide options may end up providing spiritual stress instead.

One way around this is to offer 'free response' time. This involves providing a wide range of materials (construction, paint, paper, pens, games, books, figures, etc.) for children to choose from. This approach allows and values the development of each child's preferred spiritual language. Children can also choose for themselves whether they want to be on their own, or with others. But when with others, they are also learning through observation about the rich variety of spiritual life, and may occasionally feel intrigued enough to try something out of their comfort zone. For adults in spiritual direction or on spiritual retreats, this step outside the comfort zone can be a breakthrough to new insight. For example, putting aside skills we feel confident in using (such as verbal analysis of a text) to explore our response through a much weaker skill (perhaps painting or role-play). Keeping these options open for when a child is ready to choose, is an important way in which different learning styles can be a route to rich spiritual life.

How do negative experiences affect children's spirituality?

Crises can offer a window on spirituality, revealing, for example, a courageous or hopeful spirit in the direst of circumstances. When the mother of a primary school child died of cancer, teachers at the school said they learned more in one week about the spiritual depths of children in their classes than years of teaching them had disclosed. In many ways the children's spiritual questions and ways of making meaning, and peace, with the tragedy helped the teachers do the same.

Crises can also develop or impair children's spirituality. Importantly, bad life experiences are not necessarily bad for spirituality; they can be catalysts for spiritual development. Children whose lives present more than a fair share of problems may be prompted to consider things from a spiritual perspective sooner, more urgently or more frequently than more fortunate youngsters. Those working with children who have a life-limiting illness often notice that they want to address the 'big questions' (What's the point of life? Who am I? What is death?). These children can stagger, even frighten, parents and sometimes clergy who can't compute that children want a way to tackle this head on, rather than accept well-intentioned protection from reality. A trip half way round the world to Disneyland is sometimes seen as preferable to supporting a child who wishes to spend time in the hospital chapel or in conversation with the chaplain. For children in crisis especially, spiritual nurture is about providing space, time to process, through imagination, relationship, intimacy and trust. Distracting them and pretending that the crisis does not exist suggests that Christian language and thought are *not* spiritual resources to help children handle their challenges. Children need the full range of language too, the vocabulary (story and imagery) that deals with comfort as well as pain, despair and anger.

How about spirituality and children who are 'different'?

At the beginning of this book there is a discussion about whether or not children's spirituality might just be a kind of middle-class churchy luxury, 'the icing on the cake' for privileged churched children so that they can get ahead in holiness and piety, a bit like hot-housing children to develop precocious skills in music or tennis. But in fact, it is apparent that the more difficult children's life circumstances are, the more spiritual sensitivity and spiritual hunger they may have. This has profound challenges for how churches work with children with special needs of different kinds.

If children have a right to have their spiritual lives taken seriously, then this applies more to children with special needs than to any others. It also seems obvious that churches should be first in the queue to offer this provision to its most vulnerable. Yet often parents are left to manage alone as church groups lack the people and specialist resources to give sufficient extra support to children with special needs. When this happens, both the child's and the parent's spiritual needs are often unmet.

It may be, however, that churches have much to learn about spirituality *from* children with special needs, such as how to appreciate non-verbal spiritual response in worship. For example, compared to others, a child with a learning difficulty may respond to a Bible story with much less inhibition and with more direct 'understanding'. While the rest of the children talked about what being part of creation meant, a boy with autism literally wrapped himself up in the long piece of material on which the picture for the seven days of creation had been laid.

There can be an assumption when working among unchurched, disadvantaged or simply Nintendo-dependent children that the best approach is high-energy, activity-packed and fun-centred. This risks missing opportunities to engage with the more complex experiences and needs these children may have. The more 'challenging' groups of children may need much less prompting to ask the big questions. Disadvantaged children of one kind or another may be more desperate to find words to ask their big questions (What can I trust? Who cares about me? What kind of person should I be and why?). In fact, it's highly likely that in some cases negative 'acting out' behaviour is their way of trying to formulate the questions and identify the parameters of the answers in the absence of suitable, spiritual, language.

This has implications for some outreach and holiday clubs. In recent times, quite rightly, care is taken to avoid offering too heavy a dose of explicit evangelization or indoctrination. But in downplaying the 'religious' element, churches have sometimes allowed a take-over by the 'keep-them-busy' and high-energy fun elements (with covert religious messages and subtle 'product placement' – 'Christians and churches are quite nice really').

The danger is that children may just not realize that they are encountering a language, Christian language, that might help them work through their personally salient spiritual concerns. For centuries, Christians have found the practices of hearing and responding to God's story, using symbol and ritual, silence and stillness, vital for connecting their lives to God's overall purposes. We need to be careful to ensure that *all* children we work with are let in on this important discovery. It must be wrong to hide this truth from certain kinds of children because Christian language has been boiled down to accessible take-home points, or because religious narrative is presented as little more than packaging for a moral code – once cracked the story is redundant.

Can troubled children's difficulties have a spiritual aspect?

Margaret Crompton writes especially about the spirituality of children who are 'in care' for one reason or another. She draws attention to the phenomenon of 'the invisible child', which can happen 'when the child's image of herself becomes cloudy and flawed . . . [they] may even feel that they do not exist and have become invisible'.[30] This invisibility is a kind of veil drawn round the child, and so can be a handicap to spirituality, to fully living and being.

Circumstances of neglect or abuse often mean that a child's only defence is to disappear under such a veil, though there can be other reasons too. Sometimes the need to become less than you are, invisible, takes obvious forms, such as elective mutism, anorexia, apathy and loss of affect, 'not caring'. These outer psychological and physical symptoms may have a significant spiritual component – signalling that this child is also in spiritual pain, cut off from being properly themselves. In some cases, the spiritual pain could originate from something quite specific. For example, dreadful guilt because they wished old Mrs Smith would die, and she did. Or a paralysing fear of death, or fear of God. Or the feeling of being locked out of peace because they are eaten up with rage or jealousy towards a new step-parent. Or experiencing a spiritual identity crisis because they don't feel they share their parents' beliefs or values, a deep sense of being 'different' and alone.

It may be tempting to hope that few of us will encounter such extremes in ministry with typical children's groups. But the incidence of children's mental health problems, and recognition of these problems, especially depressive illnesses, has markedly increased in recent years. In any case, the 'invisible child'/spiritual pain phenomenon may be more usefully considered as a spectrum on which many children can be located at one point or another. Among the children you know there may be a child who is just a bit 'invisible'. Have you ever wondered why?

Sometimes the invisible child's angst is just ignored – after all it doesn't fit in with the group 'fun' or contribute positively to the group ethos. For some children, becoming 'invisible' may be a strategy to hide from the pressure of the group dynamic of jolly Christian cheerfulness. Imagine what happens if you are the child who connects intimately to the angry dark reality of the Flood, while the rest blithely see Noah's story as a message about God's kindness to animals and knack for beautiful rainbows? Being coerced to 'join in' could be the worst thing for such children, who fear that their 'different' but fragile grasp on spirituality will be exposed or they will be forced to concede to the majority view. Bottling up their response might appear to us as non-compliance, becoming anti-social or rejection of the Christian mindset. In fact, their behaviour might arise from an especially thoughtful connection with the biblical material.

Can children's spiritual life have bad times too? Is it all positive?

It is reasonable to suppose that most children go through versions of what adults experience as 'dark night of the soul' pain. This is about becoming aware of a kind of spiritual void, when what was once a resource or meaningful loses that function. It can be a profound experience of loneliness or disappointment.

As children experience some quite dramatic shifts in their thinking, there will be times when what used to hold together stops doing that, leaving them, hopefully temporarily, with 'nothing'. For example, when the spiritual world view they had worked out as five-year-olds is no longer tenable to their ten-year-old minds. For children, this might be especially lonely as they can't know what's happening or how to ask for help. It can also be confusing. Children can report feeling embarrassed by the 'silliness' of the spirituality of their younger selves, even questioning their sanity.[31] They do not know how to handle changes in their spiritual perception and attitude.

The nurture of children needs to address the reality of spiritual emptiness and spiritual transition, especially in later childhood, as much as it values and supports their spiritual vitality. Sadly, this is rarely a topic we feel confident to pursue with children – as if to open it up will make it happen. Our silence compounds their sense of loneliness and we hide from them the rich spiritual language of the Christian tradition that deals exactly with experiences of God's absence, with doubt and with feeling confused.

Who should take primary responsibility for children's spirituality? Whose job is this anyway? Parents? Leaders of the children's work? The wider Church?

Your own spiritual life is probably quite a personal matter, something you may prefer to share with only a few selected confidantes. It is likely that children feel the same most of the time. This raises the question of whether church is an appropriate place for attending to spirituality. It might seem that this calls for such high standards of intimacy, trust and relatedness that only a home setting can provide adequately for children's spirituality. So is it primarily a job for parents?

In an ideal world, perhaps this would be the case, but of course not all children have parents available or able to fulfil this role. Even for those who do, it can be disturbing to have to switch between spiritual cultures – if, for example, at home a child's spiritual questions (and ways of asking those) are taken seriously, whereas at church they are more likely to be set aside as interruptions. Parents and other special friends who might offer children more individual attention for their spirituality are invaluable, but this task implies a much wider set of responsibilities than simply those of family and friends.

The local church has a central role to play in nurturing children's spirituality. The size of this responsibility is not always appreciated. Whereas the minister or clergy take primary responsibility for the spiritual nurture of the adult congregation, the children's work leaders are required to carry out this function for the children. Normally these are untrained volunteers, so it is quite understandable that some children's group leaders may have a relatively narrow sense of their task, and may or may not recognize how fundamental spirituality is.

All this suggests a chain of responsibility approach: those with theological and pastoral training need to give detailed support to those who are acting on their behalf as 'clergy to the children', equipping them to understand the breadth and depth of that ministry. In other words, it is not enough to ask someone to look after or teach the children, allocate a small budget and offer a few words of thanks from time to time. The spiritual challenges of the job need to be explored and supported, both in terms of human spirituality and the spirituality of teaching, topics about which those with theological training ought to have a well-developed knowledge.

The extent to which those in authority (clergy, ministers) lead by example should not be underestimated, either. The attitude and behaviour they take towards children's spiritual capacities will often influence the approach of parents and children's leaders, without either knowing it! Observing one another's style, and making time to talk about it, might be a very useful discussion indeed.

Lastly, children's spirituality is a responsibility of the wider Church too. As children's lives seem increasingly pressured, and childhood itself seems under threat, the Church has a duty to speak out for the spiritual significance of child and childhood. This task might include reaching well outside its doors and its own children, to call attention to practices and attitudes generally that endanger children's spirituality by their indifference to the value of space, process, imagination, relationship, intimacy and trust.

Further reading and resources

This book has tried to offer as simple a guide as possible to a complex area. The following would be helpful to any who would like to explore this area in more depth.

Jerome W. Berryman, *The Complete Guide to Godly Play*, vol. 1, Living the Good News, 2002 (see also vols 2–6 for stories to tell, etc)
Handbooks to inform practitioners in the art of using Godly Play in church and other settings.

Jerome W. Berryman, *Godly Play: An Imaginative Approach to Religious Education*, Augsburg Fortress, 1995
An introduction to Godly Play and the story of its development.

Sofia Cavalletti, *The Religious Potential of the Child*, translated by J. M. Coulter and P. M. Coulter, Paulist Press, 1983
A beautiful account of years of careful observation of young children doing Montessori-style Christian education in Italy.

Robert Coles, *The Spiritual Life of Children*, HarperCollins, 1990
A rich tapestry of conversations the author had with children from all kinds of religious backgrounds. Leaves a deep impression of their spirituality, but has less to suggest about the practical implications.

Kathryn Copsey, *From the Ground Up: Understanding the Spiritual World of the Child*, Barnabas, 2005
Based on the author's many years of experience working with children in the inner city, this is a very readable guide to thinking about children's spirituality in almost any context.

David Hay with Rebecca Nye, *The Spirit of the Child*, HarperCollins, 1998 (Jessica Kingsley Publications, revised edition, 2006)
An account of an in-depth research study interviewing British schoolchildren about their richly spiritual lives. Includes a thorough treatment of previous literature in the area and reflection on how easily children's spirituality is

undermined by current trends in education.

International Journal of Children's Spirituality, Carfax Publishing, from 1996 to the present day
An academic, peer-reviewed journal with articles on all aspects of children's spirituality. Often more secular in emphasis.

Janet Marshall Eibner and Susan Graham Walker, *God, Kids and Us: The Growing Edge of Ministry with Children and the People Who Care for Them*, Morehouse Publishing, 1996
A superbly practical guide to rethinking how you approach children's ministry, lots of exercises to do as a team and some classic anecdotes.

Donald Ratcliff (ed.), *Children's Spirituality: Christian Perspectives, Research and Applications*, Cascade Books, 2004
A collection of articles written in an academic style but includes an article by Rebecca Nye about researching spirituality.

Fraser Watts, Rebecca Nye and Sara Savage, *Psychology for Christian Ministry*, Routledge, 2001
A comprehensive textbook covering many aspects of ministry for the non-psychologist church worker, includes chapters on faith development, child and adolescent psychology, applying educational theories, personality and social factors.

Gretchen Wolff-Pritchard, *Offering the Gospel to Young Children*, Cowley Publications, 1992
A classic treatise on how the Bible can be used authentically with children. A manifesto for treating both the Bible and children with deep respect and acknowledging the complexity of both.

Web sites
Association for Children's Spirituality
www.childrenspirituality.org

Godly Play UK
www.godlyplay.org.uk
Includes details about training courses and practical introductions to this approach, consultancy and how to access materials to use in your own setting. Contact details for Rebecca Nye can be found here too.

About children in theological perspective

Jerome Berryman, *Godly Play: An Imaginative Approach to Religious Education*, Augsburg Fortress, 1995
The final chapter especially tackles the theological implications of the Godly Play's understanding of Christian nurture.

Marcia J. Bunge (ed.), *The Child in Christian Thought*, Eerdmans, 2001
A fine collection of contemporary essays about major theologians who have addressed childhood through the centuries.

David H. Jensen, *Graced Vulnerability: A Theology of Childhood*, Pilgrim Press, 2005
Accessible and profound.

Joyce Mercer, *Welcoming Children: A Practical Theology of Childhood*, Chalice Press, 2005
Scholarly and wide ranging, informed by feminist theory, offers a valuable practical theology of childhood and Christian education.

Bonnie J. Miller-McLemore, *Let the children Come: Re-imagining Childhood from a Christian Perspective*, John Wiley and Sons, 2003
Combines an academic approach with reflection on the author's experience, especially as a mother.

Karl Rahner, 'Ideas for a Theology of Childhood', in *Theological Investigations, vol. 8: Further Theology of the Spiritual Life 2*, translated by David Bourke, Herder & Herder, 1971
A short article by a heavy-weight Roman Catholic theologian with enough ideas and challenges to fill a library! Essential reading.

Anne Richards and Peter Privett (eds), *Through the Eyes of a Child: New Insights in Theology from a Child's Perspective*, Church House Press, 2009
A uniquely British contribution to this area. A collection of essays by a variety of UK authors from a range of denominations. Each chapter draws on the experience or interpretation that children themselves lend to each theological theme.

Rowan Williams, *Lost Icons*, T&T Clark, 2000
The Archbishop of Canterbury's perspective on childhood and choice in the first chapter is well worth reading.

Notes

1. This was what struck me about my five-week-old son. His natural talent for 'just being' was overwhelming. Maybe it's not a bad shortlist, either, of what spirituality entails at any age.

2. See David Hay with Rebecca Nye, *The Spirit of the Child*, HarperCollins, 1998 (revised edition, Jessica Kingsley Publications, 2006).

3. This happened in the ways 'moral development' was defined and thought about. For some time, its characteristics were based on research that had only considered male experiences. When Carol Gilligan ran her research studies with women, it transpired that a whole dimension of morality had been overlooked.

4. Kalevi Tamminen, *Religious Development in Childhood and Youth: An Empirical Study*, Suomalainen Tiedeakatemia Publishers, 1991.

5. See Edward Robinson, *The Original Vision: A Study of the Religious Experience of Childhood*, Seabury Press, 1983.

6. This is probably true for adults too. We may feel more comfortable opening up outside the church context – in a cell or home group, for example.

7. See David Hay with Rebecca Nye, *The Spirit of the Child*.

8. Ana-Maria Rizzuto, *The Birth of a Living God: A Psychoanalytic Study*, University of Chicago Press, 1979, p. 10.

9. David Hay with Rebecca Nye, *The Spirit of the Child*.

10. See Jerome Berryman, *The Complete Guide to Godly Play*, vol. 1, Living the Good News, 2002.

11. It can be helpful to visit a nearby Godly Play room to see for yourself how a space for children can embody Christian spiritual life. 'Model' rooms include those in Oxford, Southwark, Guildford, Wakefield, Middlesbrough and Sheffield dioceses. See www.godlyplay.org.uk for contact details.

12. Though it is likely that to the disciples' ears the Lord's Prayer was quite a breakthrough in not being too formulaic, it was a 'form', nevertheless.

13. Alice Miller, *The Drama of Being a Child: The Search for the True Self*, Virago, 1995.

14. This can be a fault in some action songs too. All the effort goes into creating funny actions for different words, but the gestures make little contribution to exploring the

emotional sense of the song, to getting inside its spiritual meaning in a way that relies less on verbal language.

15. A view practitioners of the Godly Play approach see confirmed by the quality of the responses children make to stories presented in this way. These stories become a language to help them make meaning in their own lives, on their own terms.

16. Note how different that is from imposing an interactive response, such as, 'I want you all to cheer when Moses and his people realize their firstborns have been spared.' Or, 'Imagine you have just made it across the parted sea with Moses – let's all shout, "Thank you, wonderful God!"' These could inhibit the exploration of a child's intuition of the suffering of the Egyptians, of the tension between God's hostility and protection, of justice and mercy.

17. Marcia J. Bunge (ed.), *The Child in Christian Thought*, Eerdmans, 2001.

18. Chris Jamber is a Godly Play trainer in the USA. This quote appeared in First Friday, the newsletter for Godly Play trainers, 2003.

19. See Sofia Cavalletti, *The Religious Potential of the Child*, Paulist Press, 1983.

20. Jerome Berryman, *The Complete Guide to Godly Play*, vol. 1, Living the Good News, 2002 (see also volumes 2–6 for stories to tell, etc) and *Godly Play: An Imaginative Approach to Religious Education*, Augsburg Fortress, 1995.

21. See David Hay with Rebecca Nye, *The Spirit of the Child*.

22. Notice the captions and images that appear on T-shirts for children: 'Mummy's little angel', 'Daddy's little monster'. What messages do they convey about our views of children? Consider also what messages these send to children.

23. Gretchen Wolff-Pritchard, *Offering the Gospel to Young Children*, Cowley Publications, 1992.

24. Karl Rahner, 'Ideas for a Theology of Childhood', in *Theological Investigations*, vol. 8, Further Theology of the Spiritual Life 2, translated by David Bourke, Herder & Herder, 1971.

25. This might be a radical alternative to the model in some churches where the children are asked to tell the congregation what they've been learning. Instead, the children's leaders might give an account of what they (the adults) have learned; or the congregation might be invited to reflect on what they have learned or become aware of through the presence of children over a period. If the objective of 'show and tell' in worship is to assure the children that they are valued by this community, both these alternatives meet that need.

26. Child development does not only identify changes in intellectual life. Stages in emotional, social and moral development are also proposed. For some psychologists,

these other domains are subject to broadly similar patterns; but for others, quite different patterns are described (e.g. Erikson on social development, Freud on emotional/personality development). Churches (following schools) have drawn mostly on theories about intellectual development, hence the focus here. For discussion of a wider range of child development issues and what these mean for faith development across the age span, see *Psychology for Christian Ministry* by Fraser Watts, Rebecca Nye and Sara Savage, Routledge, 2001.

27. David Hay with Rebecca Nye, *The Spirit of the Child.*

28. Peter L. Berger, *A Rumour of Angels: Modern Society and the Recovery of the Supernatural*, Allen Lane/Penguin Press, 1970.

29. See also, James W. Fowler, Karl Ernst Nipkow and Friedrich Schweitzer (eds), *Stages of Faith and Religious Development: Implications for Church*, Education and Society, SCM Press, 1991.

30. Margaret Crompton, *Children, Spirituality, Religion and Social Work*, Ashgate, 1998.

31. See David Hay with Rebecca Nye, *The Spirit of the Child.*

Index

non-verbal conveyance of value of
children   43–4
prayer in   57–64 *see also* prayer
process-centred vs. production-centred
46–8
responsibility for   94–5
role recognition and evaluation in   83–4
and the sense of intimacy   53–4
special needs children and   91–2
trust and   55–6
see also teaching
Church
attention to space   42–3
child-friendly vs. child-spirituality-friendly
practices   20, 48
children's ministry *see* children's
ministry
church buildings and spirituality   42–4
importance of children's spirituality for
the Church   16–19
non-verbal conveyance of value of
children   43–4, 73–4
resources   43
responsibility for children's spirituality
94–5
special needs children and   91–2
worship *see* worship
communication
auditory space and   45
candid comments from children on
conventional spirituality   28–31
children's adaptation to social demands
of   27–8
a child's 'spiritual voice'   32–3, 74
discernment of heartfelt communication
28, 32–3
hearing and responding to a child's
spirituality   31–3
imaginative   49–50
language *see* language

non-verbal   27 *see also* non-verbal
elements of spirituality
questioning *see* questioning
by silence   45
'talk less, listen more' principle   27, 45
wondering and   38–9
craft   47
creation   29–30
creativity
creative play   78–9
imagination and   49–50
spiritual processing in art and craft   47
Crompton, Margaret   92

Dixon, David   3
Donaldson, Margaret   3

emotional space   44–5
Erikson, Eric   20
Erricker, Clive   3

faith, spirituality as essential to   18
feelings
childhood and   8
focus on   32
listening to   31–2
recapture of   25
sensitivity to the feel of a place   42
spirituality and   28, 29–30, 84
free response time   89
Freud, Sigmund   86

gender, and childhood spirituality   88–9
God
dark images of   80
emotional space and the immanence
and transcendence of   45
knowing/encountering God   84, 87
presence of   9, 42, 58, 59, 60, 75, 85
Godly Play   38, 64

CPSIA information can be obtained at www.ICGtesting.com
Printed in the USA
LVOW05s1640180814

PP8728900001B/1/P